Five One-Act Plays
on Ideological Fanaticism

by Marvin Perry, Ph.D.

DORRANCE
PUBLISHING CO
EST. 1920
PITTSBURGH, PENNSYLVANIA 15238

Dorrance Publishing Co
585 Alpha Drive
Pittsburgh, PA 15238
Visit our website at *www.dorrancebookstore.com*

ISBN: 978-1-6480-4345-1
eISBN: 978-1-6480-4369-7

TABLE OF CONTENTS

PREFACE

In my books on modern intellectual history, antisemitism, and World War II, it was necessary to discuss why people embraced irrational ideas, myths that fostered fanaticism and ultimately proved dangerous for society and even civilization. I have attempted to treat these themes within a dramatic setting.

The five one-act plays in this volume explore the theme of ideological fanaticism. Three of the plays deal with Nazi Germany, the classic example of this phenomenon. The remaining two plays treat contemporary examples of ideological fanaticism, jihadism and white supremacy. In writing the plays, I have tried to probe within a dramatic context, the thinking and feelings of Nazis (and their opponents), Islamic jihadists, and white supremacists, true believers propelled to commit and to justify atrocities against people they designate as the "other". Each play is preceded by a brief introduction that provides the reader with an historical frame of reference.

The plays do not have to be performed. They can simply be read for the ideas they contain and as the basis of a discussion. If they are to be performed, they lend themselves to small casts composed of readers who do not have to memorize parts or leave their seats. Only one play requires more than four participants. Of course, a director can arrange productions in which the performers are not reading but acting on a stage.

I hope you find the plays informative and appealing.

M.P.

GERMAN VETERANS TORMENTED BY THE DARK PAST

Historical Introduction

It would take decades for Germans to come to terms with their Nazi past. After the war, they were reluctant to talk about it, especially to their children, or they displayed a selective memory. Several developments compelled Germans to face responsibility. By the mid-1960s, a new generation of educators began to teach and discuss the Nazi years, breaking with older instructors, many of them former Nazi Party members who simply avoided the subject. And a new generation of students began to press parents and teachers to describe what happened during the Nazi years, including their own behavior. They were stirred by the trial in Jerusalem of Adolf Eichmann, who supervised the deportation of European Jews to the death camps, and the trial in Frankfort of the SS administration at Auschwitz. Both trials provided mountains of evidence, including the horrifying testimonies of many survivors of Nazi torture and assembly-line murder.

In the closing decades of the twentieth century scholars, many of them Germans, dispelled the myths predominating in postwar

Germany that had given Germans psychological comfort. Particularly distressing for Germans was the debunking of the myth that the Wehrmacht, the regular army, unlike the SS, was untainted by war crimes. Since the millions of men who served in the Wehrmacht were drawn from all classes and sections of the population, proving that it participated in individual and organized acts of persecution and mass murder—and the evidence is overwhelming—would be an indictment of the entire nation. No doubt this caused some Wehrmacht veterans, and maybe even a few former SS, to reflect on their behavior in the dark past.

Today Germans, including clergy, lament the evil that had gripped a past generation and the misery that these Germans had brought to Germany and Europe. They still ponder how a culturally advanced nation could regress to preposterous racial thinking and engage in such barbaric behavior. The Nazi era is now an important part of Germany's school and university curricula and public discourse.

Narrator, "scene 1: around 1995, fifty years after the end of WW II, Karl and Elsa, a German couple are having coffee."

Karl

"Is coffee ready?"

Elsa

"Here it is, just as you like it. How did you sleep last night?"

Karl

"As usual, not good."

Elsa

"You've been like that ever since you saw that exhibit on the Wehrmacht."

Karl

"True. The 'Crimes of the Wehrmacht' exhibit has toured Germany attracting large audiences. I find it very upsetting. The photographs of atrocities and the commentary by historians and interviews with veterans, shamed me. I can't seem to get over it."

Elsa

"We've been told over and over again that criminal Nazi leaders and the fanatic SS committed the atrocities. These were evil people. But the Wehrmacht, in which you served, fought bravely and had clean hands—right?"

Karl

"The exhibit did not deal with the SS but with the criminal behavior of the Wehrmacht. Unlike the SS, the Wehrmacht was not an elite force of dedicated Nazis, many of them volunteers, but our nation's army. Millions of men from all over the country, me included, served in it. And it did not have clean hands."

Elsa

"Haven't we had enough with the Nazi past? We've paid billions of dollars in reparations and our schools now teach about the Holocaust. Do our critics ever think about the deliberate bombing of German civilians and the destruction of our cities? Or the deportation of hundreds of thousands of Germans to the Soviet gulag where most died? And what about the mass rape of our women by the Russians?"

Karl

"Of course, millions of Germans suffered, but it was Hitler's war. He wanted it and started it and most of us remained loyal to the bitter end. And the Wehrmacht, not just the SS, committed great crimes. The memory of these crimes constantly tortures me."

Elsa

"Karl, you were a German soldier fighting for his country. I'm sure you never killed innocents or Jews like the SS did. But in all the years since the war you have refused to discuss your experiences with me or Josef, although your medals showed your bravery. I'm sure you have nothing to hide. Have you spoken to our son recently?"

Karl

"I am not proud of these medals. Josef pleaded with me to attend the exhibit. While some right-wing zealots and some veterans have been critical, he said, it has gained overwhelming praise."

Elsa

"Did you discuss the exhibit with him? You know of course that Josef is a history professor who knows a great deal about the Nazi years. It would be good for your head to speak with your son."

Karl

"You're probably right, but I just cannot do it."

Elsa

"I hate to see you tortured by the past. The war ended 50 years ago. We're a different country now and this is a different era. And I'm certain you served honorably, even though you won't tell me about it."

Karl

"Thanks for your kind words. I'm meeting Hans for lunch. I'll see you later."

Narrator, "scene 2: Karl and Hans talking."

Karl

"As always, it's good to see you. Are you still struggling with retirement?"

Hans

"I'm adjusting better. What really works for me are the courses I started taking at the university. I never was much of a scholar, but reading first-rate books and listening to lectures, some by brilliant professors, has opened up a new world for me."

Karl

"The last time we met you said you were really moved by your courses on German literature and classical music. I was impressed. What are you taking now?"

Hans

"It was difficult for me to enroll in a course on Nazi Germany, but I bit the bullet and did it. I told myself, just listen and never comment."

Karl

"How is your professor?"

Hans

"Superb. He knows the facts and focuses on significant events but also on the meaning of the Nazi experience for Germans, Jews and for all those who want to understand the madness that engulfed our nation. But first, give me your reaction to the exhibit on Wehrmacht crimes."

Karl

"I participated in several actions similar to those shown in the exhibit. In reprisal for partisan attacks, my unit alone killed many Russian hostages. Because supplies of food and warm clothing often reached us late, we confiscated the peasants' crops and warm winter clothing. And when we needed housing for our patrols we drove peasants out into the sub-zero weather, condemning them to death by hunger and cold."

Hans

"The propaganda circulating among the troops portrayed the Russians as a lower and brutal form of humanity. And we burned thousands of villages to the ground."

Karl

"My unit took part in this crime, liquidating hundreds of villages. We killed many of the peasants outright; others, without shelter or food, could not survive the winter."

Hans

"Are you still tormented by the memory?"

Karl

"As much as I try I cannot forget or rationalize my behavior."

Hans

"I have the same problem."

Karl

"A particular incident has kept me in agony for years. My unit was ordered to assist the Einsatzgruppen in rounding up Jews for mass slaughter. What kind of people were we to organize mobile SS murder squads whose sole purpose was to slaughter Jews?"

Hans

"My professor says they massacred with gunfire some 1.3 million Jews, including children, in what they called cleansing operations."

Karl

"In a couple of towns, we helped round up a sizeable number of Soviet Jews who were sent to execution grounds a short distance away. One 10-year old boy said to me in perfect German: 'Please sir we are good people. My ancestors came from Germany.' A group of us managed to witness the slaughter. There I saw the young boy and his family among others lined up at the edge of a large pit. I turned away as the machine gunner did his evil work."

Hans

"As you know I was in an SS unit stationed in the Warsaw Ghetto. We crammed a few hundred thousand Jews from all over Poland into a small area of the city and built a ten-foot wall topped with barbed wire to seal them in. Living conditions were horrendous—brutal congestion and little food or medical care. We shot any Jew who tried to escape the ghetto, including young children who would crawl through a breach in the wall in order to bring food back to their starving families."

Karl

"I recall reading that starving the Jews to death became official policy."

Hans

"Yes, the higher ups even boasted of the numbers who perished from starvation. We soon reduced the Jews to a handful of calories a day. Every day Jewish forced laborers picked up emaciated bodies from the streets. We killed over 300,000 Jews in the ghetto by rampant starvation, disease, gunshot, and eventually the gas chambers at Treblinka. For our officials, gassing, which could kill thousands of Jews a day, was the most effective way of realizing the Party's policy of completely and quickly annihilating the Warsaw Ghetto."

Karl

"Did you participate in the hunt for child smugglers?"

Hans

"That I followed orders to shoot these desperate children will always tear me apart. After killing two boys, probably about ten years old, I never again went for a kill. This angered the officer in charge. He attributed it to poor marksmanship and ordered me to practice my shooting."

Karl

"Did you assist in the herding of Jews into cattle cars to be gassed at Treblinka. You don't have to tell me."

Hans

"Yes. But I soon did everything I could to get out of it. My dedication to Nazism had completely dissipated. Are we fighting to shoot children and to murder entire families in death camps I asked myself? Are those SS men who make a game of shooting Jews for target practice in the ghetto streets representative of the new Germany? Only a German defeat could save the country."

Karl

"Did you feel like a traitor when you thought that way?"

Hans

"When I did feel that I was turning against my country and my comrades, I told myself that defeat would liberate the German people from the criminals who ran the government, brought us into this terrible war, and considered the extermination of Jews, including children, a key national policy. Ridding Germany of Hitler and his Nazis was my country's only hope."

Karl

"Did you ever help a Jew in the Ghetto?"

Hans

"I tried. When no one was looking, I passed food to starving street children. This could be dangerous. Our police would shoot a Pole who gave a piece of bread to a starving Jewish child smuggled out of the ghetto; they would also shoot the child. I did kill a Jew who worked for the Nazis reporting wanted Jews in hiding. No regrets. One time I confronted an SS who routinely beat Jews with his rifle butt as they assembled for the cattle cars taking them to Treblinka."

Karl

"What could you have said to make him stop?"

Hans

"I asked him if it were necessary to inflict more pain on these poor souls being deported to the gas chambers. He replied in Nazi language that 'Jews are vermin who don't deserve to live.' I pointed to a mother hugging two children and asked: 'what would your mother say if she saw you taking pleasure in beating a mother protecting her children?'"

Karl

"What did he do?"

Hans

"I don't know what went through his mind, but he simply brought the rifle to his side and walked away."

Karl

"You took a chance. He could have reported you. I also underwent a transformation after participating in the horrific persecution of Russian civilians and watching the Einsatzgruppen round up and systematically murder large numbers of Jews. I and another soldier, who also was repelled by Nazi cruelty, tried not to burn every house in a village and did not take all of a peasant family's food and warm clothing. We were fortunate that no one noticed."

Hans

"There is one incident I experienced 20 years after the war that compounds my misery."

Karl

"After the war! That's intriguing."

Hans

"I had broken my left arm and the nurse who was fitting me with a cast spotted the SS blood tattoo on the inside of the upper arm. 'SS,' she said, her face and eyes burning with hatred. 'I have a tattoo too.' She lifted up her sleeve and showed the number we tattooed on concentration camp inmates and said: 'Auschwitz, the SS gassed my parents, my brothers and sisters, and 25 relatives.' And then she spat in my face, and walked away."

Karl

"Did you report her?"

Hans

"Yeah, sure. I could see the headline in a tabloid. Former SS man seeks justice for abuse by a female Jewish survivor of Auschwitz."

Karl

"Speaking about the postwar. Did you ever attend meetings of SS veterans that were held regularly for years after the war?"

Hans

"For a while I did, but soon became outraged by their behavior. They looked back fondly at Nazi victories and sang Nazi marches with spirit; in unison, they chanted *Sieg Heil* and gave the Nazi salute. Speaker after speaker praised SS heroism and criticized Germans who denounced their conduct. There is no doubt that they still relished Nazi doctrines and power and several revealed their ongoing adulation for Hitler."

Karl

"Did they ever show any remorse?"

Hans

"They were rich in denials, rationalizations, even justifications. But I never saw remorse. They even made jokes about the gassing of Jews. I attended a reunion where a former SS general, addressing SS veterans, removed from his pocket a gas-filled cigarette lighter allowing the gas to escape slowly. 'What is that?' he asked sniffing it, and then he gave his reply: 'A Jew nostalgic for Auschwitz.' The audience laughed. I was infuriated and never went to another meeting." *Narrator: "This incident is documented."*

Karl

"Back to your course. It must be painful for you to listen and read about how we nearly destroyed Western civilization."

Hans

"The course has compelled me to relive and reflect on my disgraceful behavior during the war. As I intended, I did not participate in discussions. But then the professor arranged for Max Cohen, a survivor of the Warsaw Ghetto, to describe his experiences. Mr. Cohen is about 70. He spoke of Jewish suffering and SS cruelty."

Karl

"Did he say anything about the uprising in the ghetto's last days?

Hans

"Yes. I was almost in tears when he recounted how the surviving Jews resisted our attempts to transport them to Treblinka. Armed with a few guns and some homemade bottled explosives, they fought our patrols for almost a month. They continued their desperate struggle as we systematically set fire and blew up block by block, building after building in the ghetto. Mr. Cohen was one of the few fighters to escape through the sewers."

Karl

"Did you say anything?"

Hans

"I didn't want to. But after Mr. Cohen's talk a student questioned whether German soldiers would deliberately shoot children. The professor said that 1,500,000 Jewish children perished in the Holocaust, many were shot by the Einsatzgruppen; others were gassed, or died of starvation, brutality, and lack of medical treatment. He examined his notes and took out a letter written by a death squad assassin to his wife in October 1941: 'Infants flew great arcs through the air, and we shot them to pieces in flight before their bodies fell into the pit.' *Narrator: "This is an actual documented incident."* Students were in shock, some even shed tears."

Karl

"And what did you say?"

Hans

"I could not contain myself. I said calmly that I was stationed in the Warsaw Ghetto. Everything Mr. Cohen said is true. I observed our soldiers hunting down and killing brave children trying to sneak food into the starving ghetto. Any Jewish child caught outside the ghetto was immediately shot. These SS never seemed troubled. Indeed, they took pride in killing these children whom they called Jew criminals. The class was totally silent and I said nothing else."

Karl

"What idiots we were to fall for Hitler and his race nonsense."

Hans

"My failure began early. Before the war I was part of gangs that beat up Jews, defaced their shops, and held signs telling people not to buy in so-called 'Jew stores'. I believed so much in Nazi racial myths that I enlisted in the SS and was filled with pride when they accepted me. I can't get over how millions of Germans, including myself, believed these stupid myths and how cruelly we behaved."

Karl

"After the war, we told the victors that we were not Nazis but victims of a government controlled by criminals. More nonsense! By 1939, the great majority of our people supported Hitler and embraced his beliefs. At the rallies I attended, the adulation for Hitler was overwhelming."

Hans

"How could people living in a highly-civilized nation, many of them with superb educations, descend so quickly and completely into barbarism? I would like to hear what your son has to say on this question. He's still at the university—right? Do you ever discuss with him the Nazis and your wartime experiences?"

Karl

"When Josef was growing up he kept asking me about the war. I always put him off. When he was at school, his teachers did not discuss the Nazi years. No doubt many

of them had things to hide. But with the trials of Eichmann and the Nazis who staffed Auschwitz, things started
to change. By the 1970s, young people showed tremen-
dous interest in Hitler, the war and Nazi war crimes. Josef
read vociferously and grew suspicious of me as I continued
to avoid his queries."

Hans

"Karl, you're getting old and Josef is a history professor.
Isn't it time you had a serious discussion with him about
the war. It might even help clear your head."

Karl

"You're right, I'm going to contact him."

Narrator, "scene 3: Karl in Josef's office."

Josef

"Hi dad, it's great to see you. I think you've only been
to my office once or twice before. How are you
doing?"

Karl

"Mother tells me to speak to you about the emotional tur-
moil I am going through."

Josef

"If you need a caring voice, I'm here. What's bothering you?"

Karl

"A couple of weeks ago I went to the exhibit on the crimes of the Wehrmacht that you recommended. I also have regular conversations with my good friend Hans—you met him once years back—about our wartime experiences. Both the exhibit and the conversations have filled me with guilt that won't go away. My mind can't bury what I witnessed and did during the war. Sleeping has become a major problem."

Josef

"I understand. While many veterans have simply buried the memory of the war, I have spoken to several veterans who are also torn apart by what they saw and did during the war."

Karl

"I'm relieved that I am not alone."

Josef

"Where were you fighting?"

Karl

"In Operation Barbarossa I was part of Army Group South that drove into the Ukraine and moved on Kiev. Our initial victories on every front were spectacular. Everywhere we were advancing, encircling, and killing and capturing vast numbers of Russians. Some villagers even greeted us as liberators from Stalin's hated communism and terror. We thought that the Red Army was near disintegration, and as in France the war with Russia would soon end."

Josef

"This must have been thrilling for you."

Karl

"Very thrilling for an immature 20-year old."

Josef

"Where were you when the war turned against us?"

Karl

"In the spring of 1944, I was in Belorussia when the Russians launched their huge offensive that soon brought them to the gates of Warsaw. In the months that followed, we continued to fight but could not match Russian manpower and armaments. I was part of a beaten and increasingly dispirited force retreating from Russia. Fortunately, I was not killed or taken prisoner by the Soviets."

Josef

"The SS and Gestapo hunted down deserters and so-called defeatists and hung them from lampposts, telephone poles, and trees with signs pinned on their clothes: 'I was too cowardly to defend my fatherland.' 'I am a deserter.' 'All traitors die like this one.' These executions were widely publicized as a warning to soldiers in the field."

Karl

"As we retreated, I saw a number of these hanged soldiers."

Josef

"Of course, I am grateful that you survived and were not imprisoned by the Soviets. But so far you have not told me about any deeds you committed that still plague your conscience. What is it that troubles you and keeps you from sleeping?"

Karl

"I never told you or your mother about my deplorable behavior. Hans is the only one who knows."

Josef

"Karl, I know talking about it with me is painful for you, but it is a necessary way of relieving your agony."

Karl

"I know you're right. But please don't judge your father as a terrible person when I tell you."

Josef

"Don't worry. I only want to help not judge."

Karl

"I participated in the shooting of numerous villagers in reprisal for partisan attacks and in stealing the peasants' food and winter clothing before sending them into the cold to die. And we burned countless villages to the ground which greatly increased the number of civilian deaths."

Josef

"The Wehrmacht was ordered to execute 100 hostages for every German soldier killed by partisans. Did you help exterminate Jews?"

Karl

"At times, I was ordered to assist in rounding up Jews for the Einsatzgruppen to slaughter. I also helped lead thousands of Russian prisoners of war to camps where it was the Wehrmacht's policy to kill them by starvation. What horror!"

Josef

"You're right; it was a horror. I'm sure you were moved by the exhibit on Wehrmacht crimes that showed the treatment of Soviet prisoners of war. Some 3 million prisoners perished, most from deliberate starvation. And these camps were not run by the SS but by our national army; for decades, we were told that the Wehrmacht committed no crimes but only fought honorably."

Karl

"I can't understand how many veterans put the war aside and just go on with their lives. They do not suffer from guilt as I do."

Josef

"They have found ways to ease their conscience. They say it was not their decision to kill innocent civilians; they were only following orders, the same words used by defendants in war crime trials. And they point to Stalin's horrendous crimes to show that they were fighting a cruel foe who threatened the fatherland. Many deny any knowledge of the Holocaust until after the war, an unlikely story. It's more believable when they say that they were too concerned with staying alive to worry about Jews. These and other rationalizations helped ease if not erase any guilt. Some feel no shame at all, but take pride in their loyalty to the fatherland and their successes on the battlefield."

Karl

"I guess it's my fate to live with guilt."

Josef

"I am not a psychologist. I don't know if I can alleviate your pain. But that you still agonize over your behavior and not just dismiss it, is to me a healthy sign. Getting others never to forget the evils of our past should ease your pain. I want to make a suggestion, I would like you to consider."

Karl

"Please go ahead."

Josef

"I'm part of a group that gives lectures and holds discussions in secondary schools, universities, and for adult groups. I could get you places to speak. Our audiences are used to academics and survivors, but they rarely hear the voice of veterans. What do you think."

Karl

"Intriguing. Could I go as a team with Hans?"

Josef

"Tell me about Hans."

Karl

"Like me he regrets serving the Nazis."

Josef

"How exactly did he serve?"

Karl

"He was SS and stationed in the Warsaw Ghetto."

Josef

"O my God! I've heard survivors talk about the Warsaw Ghetto, but never an SS veteran. He would generate great interest."

Karl

"Could the three of us meet next week and work on a method of procedure?"

Josef

"How about a week from today at the same time?"

Karl

"Sounds good. I'll check with Hans."

Narrator, "scene 4: Karl, Hans, and Josef."

Karl

"Hi son. This is Hans, a dear friend. We are excited about your proposal."

Josef

"Welcome. Please sit down. Let's get right to what I have in mind. I would like the two of you, both veterans, to give talks on the war before various groups and lead discussions. I am part of a team that does this and with much success.

Listening to German veterans who fought on the Eastern front would stir and educate many people for whom the war is a distant memory or even ancient history."

Karl

"But we are not trained academics. How do we proceed?"

Josef

"I have drawn up a list of topics that I will help prepare you to talk on and discuss. We'll go over an approach very carefully. After a few sessions together, your confidence will soar; you will be ready."

Hans

"We do not want the audience to view us as war criminals, even murderers of women and children."

Josef

"I understand completely. I will introduce you and tell the audience that both of you engaged in actions that still torment you. They'll understand that this is not an investigation of war crimes, but a sincere attempt of veterans to explain their behavior under the Nazi regime. And if an action against civilians were particularly cruel, instead of saying you participated in the action, just say you either witnessed or heard about it from a comrade who was there."

Hans

"I'll buy that."

Josef

"Now let's draw up a list of topics that will appeal to the audience. I would like to concentrate on the evil myths that captivated Germans before and during the war and on the new myths about the Nazi years that were embraced after the war in order to absolve Germans of guilt. But always try to personalize your comments. Your audience anticipates hearing a thoughtful and troubled veteran not a history professor. They want you to reveal your own experiences and how you reacted to them."

Karl

"The myth of the Wehrmacht's clean hands discredited in the exhibit, is a natural topic, particularly since the exhibit has aroused extraordinary interest throughout the country."

Hans

"Yes, we can treat the abuses of the military we witnessed and experienced. I have much to say on this. The audience will be captivated and saddened by our testimony. But we have to be careful not to appear as war criminals."

Karl

"I'm excited about discussing Nazi propaganda. Before the war, my teachers and school books indoctrinated us with

Hitler's ideology and Goebbels' propaganda. We were taught that it was a law of nature that the Germans, as a superior race, were entitled to expand their territory and rule others. Many teachers taught that Jews were an evil race that threatened Germany."

Hans

"Same in my classes."

Karl

"I have a story told to me by my sister which shows the ridiculousness of education in the Third Reich. It occurred in her school when Jews could still attend. One day the school was assigned an official described as a race expert; all the girls were required to attend his lecture in the auditorium. The speaker said that Germans belonged to a high race destined to rule the world, while Jews belonged to a low race that embodied evil."

Josef

"The Nazis were relentless in provoking Jew-hatred among the young."

Karl

"He then called up a girl whom he said had all the signs of a pure German Aryan–high forehead, slender figure beautiful blue eyes, and blond hair. The audience started to giggle and then burst into laughter. She's a Jewess shouted students. The principal got up quickly silenced the audience and thanked the speaker for his enlightening talk; clearly embarrassed, he quickly left the room." *Narrator: "This incident is documented."*

Josef

"That is hilarious and revealing! In my research, I came across another revealing account of the power and stupidity of Nazi racism. In France after the Allied landings, a wounded German prisoner—he might have been SS—was told by an American doctor he needed a blood transfusion. The soldier agreed as long as it was not Jewish blood. The doctor said Americans make no such distinction and without the transfusion you'll die. He chose death." *Narrator: "This incident is documented."*

Karl

"Somewhere we should point out the absurdity of the myth of Jewish inferiority."

Josef

"An important point. German Jews were the most creative minority in Europe. When Hitler came to power there were 500,000 Jews in Germany, about one percent of the population. Yet these so-called racial inferiors accounted for 32 percent of Germany's Nobel Prize winners, mainly in medicine, mathematics, and science."

Hans

"My instructor enumerated Jewish intellectual and cultural accomplishments prior to the war. Utterly extraordinary."

Karl

"During the war in Russia, officers told us that Jews were dangerous sub-humans who deserved any suffering we inflicted on them. We were told to see ourselves as noble idealists doing humanity a service by crushing the Jews and destroying their international conspiracy to dominate the world."

Josef

"This idea of powerful and wealthy Jews conspiring to dominate the planet was quite common in Europe. It is of course pure nonsense. If Jews were so powerful, how come they couldn't get one country to bomb the gas chambers at Auschwitz?"

Hans

"In the Warsaw Ghetto, my comrades articulated the myths of Jewish inferiority and international conspiracy. These ridiculous but emotionally appealing myths led my comrades to justify deportation, starvation, and extermination. I'll need a little time to describe the horrors we inflicted on the Jews in Warsaw."

Karl

"These myths certainly were widespread among us fighting in Russia as were Nazi beliefs about the racial inferiority of Slavs."

Josef

"After the war, German generals spread the myth that they were honorable, professional soldiers who took no part in war crimes and had no knowledge of the genocide of the Jews. In recent years, researchers have uncovered much evidence that German generals ordered the plundering and destruction of thousands of Russian villages. They certainly knew about the Holocaust and even assisted the murderers. For example, in the Crimea, Field Marshal von Manstein's staff provided transport and supplies to the Einsatzgruppen death squads, which massacred some 90,000 Jews in the region."

Karl

"I am intrigued with the mind and behavior of Germans on the home front. Immediately after Hitler gained power, we were taught that Hitler was a man of destiny and a savior of the nation. The German people were spellbound by their fuehrer. Like most Germans, I considered it a duty to serve our leader and the Nazi state."

Josef

"I have just written a book on the topic of German civilians and the Third Reich. You are quite right. Many Germans did embrace Hitler, the man, his ideology, and the policies of the Third Reich."

Karl

"My family and friends witnessed the persecution and deportation of our Jewish neighbors and said nothing. I even saw some mocking the Jews as they were shoved into trucks and then railway cars to be sent to concentration camps or ghettos, mainly in Poland, where most would perish."

Josef

"Germans benefitted considerably from the plight of the Jews, virtually stealing Jewish homes, possessions, financial assets, and businesses. The theft of Jewish property throughout occupied Europe has been called the greatest economic crime in modern history. And it was not just theft. Leading companies looked to use Jewish slave labor; some firms were commissioned to build the gas chambers and cremation ovens."

Karl

"We can bring this up with the audience if questions are raised and opinions offered. But we must always remember the focus has to be on our own experiences and how we reacted to them."

Hans

"I agree that our talk has to be personalized. We are not giving a history lesson. Yet I'm sure I speak for Karl when I say we hope to stir the audience to think critically about the German past and to correct any misconceptions they still might harbor. For me, this is atonement, however limited."

Karl

"I am in total agreement. What do you think about working into the discussion following our talk with the key ideas we have drawn from our Nazi experience?"

Josef

"Excellent! The larger meaning you draw from your personal experience could have a profound effect on the audience's understanding of the Nazi years."

Karl

"A major lesson that stays with me is the ease with which German people abandoned rational thought and embraced absurd and dangerous beliefs. How could our nation be so deluded by Nazi racist ideology that defies reason?"

Josef

"Ideas and beliefs do not have to be true to win people over especially if they arouse the emotions."

Hans

"Yes, Nazi myths had a powerful effect on the SS in Warsaw. Most of my comrades were true believers driven by a utopian vision of a new world order founded on the fantasy of German racial superiority. They believed the Nazi myth that the Jews were biological trash, yet immensely evil, powerful, and dangerous enemies of the fatherland. They were convinced that ridding the world of Jews made sense and was morally justifiable."

Josef

"Nicely phrased. Even highly educated Germans became devout followers of Hitler. Did you know that a number of Einsatzgruppen assassins had college degrees even Ph.Ds?"

Karl

"I am eager to read my son's book."

Josef

"In my book, I cite the words of a Nazi doctor who helped select those Jews that would be immediately sent to the gas chambers. These poor souls had just been disgorged from crammed cattle cars after riding for days with virtually no food or water. Several Jews would die in the cars during the tortuous journey. Club-wielding SS, with dogs trained to be cruel at their side, awaited them as did the doctor doing what he considered his duty. He was consumed by race doctrines that he believed were supported by the laws of biology."

Karl

"He saw no conflict between selecting Jews to be gassed and the Hippocratic Oath?"

Josef

"The Nazi doctor was asked by a Jewish physician-inmate how he could reconcile extermination with the Hippocratic Oath he took to preserve life. Let me read the doctor's reply: 'Of course I am a doctor and I want to preserve life. And out of respect for human life I would remove a gangrenous appendix from a diseased body. The Jew is the gangrenous appendix in the body of mankind.'" *Narrator: "This quotation is documented."*

Karl

"It is beyond me how a whole nation was captivated by lies and evil myths. Another thought that stays with me is how easily human beings can descend into barbarism. What we did to Russian civilians and prisoners of war and of course, to the Jews, is a horrid break with civilized behavior. I've been reading about the concentration camps. The sadistic behavior of the guards towards Jewish inmates was beyond barbarism. Hitler's racial theories converted many of us not just into fools but depraved fools."

Hans

"The Nazi's enduring legacy is unredeemable evil. And Auschwitz, the symbol of civilization's collapse, would, sadly, join Beethoven and Goethe as an indelible component of Germany's heritage."

Josef

"Hans, you expressed this telling insight with eloquence. We must always guard against any Nazi revival, and stifle these obnoxious Holocaust deniers who are immersed in Nazi anti-Semitism. Perhaps at our next meeting both of you will have extended your thoughts on the meaning of the Nazi years to you. One question I would like you to confront is: how does the Holocaust affect the attitude of Germans and Jews toward each other?"

Karl

"How could Jews forgive us?"

Josef

"A good question. We'll look into it. I'm so glad we got this off the ground. It's going to be an important program. The next step is for me to line up schools, clubs, churches and other places that will be eager to have you. And then to work with you on the preparation."

Hans

"I'm eager to start."

Karl

"So am I."

END

Heroic German Wives, 1943

Historical Introduction

By 1943, almost all Jews who had not fled Germany while there was still a chance had been deported to slave labor camps in Germany or death camps in Poland. Jews married to non-Jews had been exempted from deportation. Many of them toiled long hours, along with other Jews whose labor was needed in vital armament factories. Now the Nazi regime was ending this policy. They wanted every Jew out of Germany. Since immigration for Jews was now prohibited, the Jews would be sent to labor camps where in a few months they would be half dead. Or they would be immediately liquidated in gas chambers in death camps set up in Poland.

Half of Germany's surviving Jews lived in Berlin. In February 1943, Joseph Goebbels, Hitler's propaganda minister and governor of Berlin, ordered the Gestapo to launch a massive roundup to rid Berlin of all Jews including the intermarried. On February 27 1943, thousands of Jews were seized and detained for speedy deportation, most likely to Auschwitz.

Jews married to "Aryans," as the Nazis defined so-called pure Germans, were placed in an old Jewish community center awaiting deportation. Their non-Jewish wives gathered in *Rosenstrasse* street in front of the building where the Gestapo and SS held their husbands and demanded their release. Over a few days, the number of demonstrators kept increasing and they would not back down even when the SS levelled machine guns at them. Aware that massacring Christian women, who only wanted their husbands back, could undermine morale at a time when Germany had just started to organize for total war, Goebbels ordered the release of the Jewish husbands.

Narrator, "scene 1: Berlin, three German women married to Jews are in anguish talking about the seizure of their Jewish husbands by the Gestapo."

Sophia

"The Nazis had already deported most Jews from Berlin. Now they want to rid Berlin of remaining Jews, even those married to Christians or Aryans as they refer to us. I'm told by my contact that in today's vast action, the Gestapo and SS arrested thousands of the city's last Jews, including children."

Ida

"They removed them from the armaments factories where they worked, grabbed them from the streets, and seized them in their homes. Numerous trucks packed with Jews kept moving through Berlin's streets. Included in the roundup were our husbands. We all thought intermarried Jews were safe. I'm furious and frightened."

Emma

"As in earlier roundups, some people turned their heads not to watch or displayed indifference. No doubt, as in other roundups, some applauded. Swallowing Goebbels' propaganda, many Germans relish the deportation of Jews, even their neighbors. Disgusting. Like earlier deportations to Poland, those just seized will wind up in camps that are killing centers. Annihilating the Jews seems to be a prime policy of our leaders."

Ida

"My friend Donna visited her son being treated in Berlin for wounds he suffered in Russia. He told her how special SS units were slaughtering Russian Jews, even women and children, by the tens of thousands. Word is circulating that in some concentration camps in Poland, the Nazis are killing vast numbers of Jews even little children in gas chambers. He said that in a camp called Auschwitz the gas chambers are very active."

Sophia

"Up to now intermarried Jews have been deferred from deportation. Our husbands were protected. But that's all over. They placed our husbands in Rosenstrasse, that old, big Jewish building on Rosenstrasse Street. The thousands of other Jews seized are in holding stations awaiting immediate deportation to camps, maybe even Auschwitz. An informant told me that the SS used horsewhips and clubs to get the Jews on and off the trucks. These sadistic bastards take pleasure in brutalizing Jews."

Emma

"These Jews will die in the camps. If we cannot save our husbands from deportation they will also wind up dead."

Sophia

"What can we do? If we protest, the Gestapo will come down hard on us."

Ida

"Maybe so. But my Jacob is a good husband and father. The Nazis already deported his parents to a concentration camp. We hope they will survive, but none of the deportees have returned. I have to do something."

Emma

"I feel the same way about Aaron."

Sophia

"I wonder what would have happened if our churches had called for mass demonstrations to stop these inhuman deportations."

Ida

"In the last couple of years, as the Nazis deported almost all German Jews east, there were no protests. The clergy behaved no better than the rest of the country; they were simply silent. No doubt some clergy even say that this is the penalty Jews have to pay for rejecting Christ."

Emma

"I don't doubt it. Even before the Nazis took power, at church I often heard priests saying hateful things about Jews in their sermons. I'm sure it was the same in Lutheran churches. I could not live with myself if I just stood by and let these evil Nazis brutalize a good man whom I love dearly."

Ida

"It's obvious that no one is going to help us. I think we would feel better if we stand outside the building on Rosenstrasse street where our husbands are being held and demand their freedom. Perhaps we will be joined by other women. But we must get there immediately."

Sophia

"You know of course that the Gestapo and SS guarding our husbands might beat and imprison us. Or, God forbid, even deport us."

Emma

"I am willing to risk it."

Ida

"Me too. We must act from the heart."

Sophia

"It gives me a good feeling to show these Nazi bastards what we think of them. Tomorrow we'll protest at Rosenstrasse."

Narrator, "scene 2: March 5, 1943, two Gestapo men stationed in Rosenstrasse discussing the women's demonstrations which have been going on for days."

Hans

"The SS are on trucks with machine guns pointed at the demonstrators. Do you think they'll fire on them?"

Siegfried

"If the women do not end their demonstrations, the SS should shoot them. These Jew-loving pigs threaten the Third Reich. We are engaged in an all-out war with the Russians. The demonstrators are internal enemies, who are hurting the war effort. If it's for the good of the fatherland we have to punish them, even kill them."

Hans

"You're right. I'm horrified that these German women insult us by living and sleeping with Jews. Shoot them!"

Siegfried

"Would you support shooting them if you had relatives in the crowd."

Hans

"As a matter of fact my sister-in-law, who is married to a Jew, a gross defiance of nature, is out there demanding her husband's release. It would not bother me in the least if we shot the bitch and the other traitors who side with the Jew enemy."

Siegfried

"They are ignorant women who have not been enlightened by what der fuehrer has said about Jews. If they knew his words they would divorce their Jewish husbands. Then the state could deal with these men just as it did with the other Jewish vermin."

Hans

"Hitler's words about the Jews have had a powerful effect on me. How perceptive is his idea that Jews are sub-humans who belong to a different species of the human race."

Siegfried

"From all I've read about Jews and from observing their behavior, I'm in total agreement with der fuehrer's belief that Jews are indelibly stained and eternally condemned by their biological makeup."

Hans

"I too am convinced that the Jews' evilness and worthlessness derive from inherited racial characteristics."

Siegfried

"Yes, and these inbred racial characteristics cannot be altered by conversion to Christianity; these racial polluters can never be German."

Hans

"Jews are fundamentally materialistic, cowardly, and treacherous. Their character traits corrupt our society. I agree with Hitler that it is vital to rid Germany of these evil and dangerous people. And we must come down hard on Aryans who protect them."

Siegfried

"The treacherous Jews have always been a hateful menace to our country. They even got Britain to bomb Berlin the other day. Goebbels was right to blame the Jews for this terror attack that killed hundreds of Berliners and left parts of the city in ruins."

Hans

"We must do everything we can to carry out Goebbels' plan to rid Berlin of all remaining Jews, including those married to Aryans. If that means deporting the husband of my wife's sister, I'd gladly push him onto the truck. I couldn't care less about what happens to him. I have no sympathy for Jews. It won't take my sister-in-law long to realize she's better off without the Jew in her house."

Siegfried

"Let's move away from talking about Jews. After the disaster at Stalingrad, people are whispering that we made a mistake invading Russia."

Hans

"We do not move away from the Jews when we talk about the war with the Soviets. Remember that Jewish communists run the country. We had to invade before the Jewish-Bolsheviks were going to attack us. The Jews would have ordered their soldiers to loot our homes, torture and murder us, and rape our women."

Siegfried

"You're right. We have to crush these Asiatic barbarians. Look how well the campaign has been going. We've conquered vast territory and killed and captured millions of the enemy."

Hans

"I know that Stalingrad hurt us. But it was only a temporary setback. With Hitler leading us, victory is certain. As Goebbels often says, our leader is a military genius."

Siegfried

"You are right! Goebbels' words are not only true, they're also inspiring. We're fortunate that Hitler has such a brilliant spokesman."

Hans

"And let's not forget what Hitler has told us over and over again: we Germans are a superior race fighting racially inferior Russians. As in all other wars the superior race is destined to win. This is a historical truth.”

Narrator, “scene 3: March 8, two other members of the Gestapo stationed at Rosenstrasse are discussing the women's protest and Goebbels' decision to release their incarcerated husbands.”

Anton

“So, Goebbels decided against deporting the intermarried Jews. They have been released. How do you explain it? I thought that ridding Berlin of Jews was a principal goal of both Goebbels, Hitler, and other Party bigwigs.”

Derek

“It's simple. The protesting wives forced his hand. On the first full day, some 200 women gathered outside the gate. In the next few days the crowd of spouses, children, and relatives swelled to nearly a thousand. The street was crammed. Most demonstrators were related to the wives of the imprisoned men, but sometimes they were joined by bystanders.”

Anton

“The women kept chanting 'We want our husbands back,' and 'Let our husbands go.' The SS held machine guns on the women and threatened to fire on them if they did not disperse. Once or twice the women scattered, but they re-gathered with greater solidarity. Spontaneously they shouted 'Murderer, Murderer' at the SS with their machine guns pointed at them. They would risk death in order to save their loved ones. What courage!"

Derek

"Remember this was not an organized protest. Women came and demonstrated on their own without any supervision."

Anton

"This forced Goebbels to back down."

Derek

"Goebbels knew he had a major problem. How would it look if the SS shot hundreds of women in Berlin because they wanted their husbands back? Goebbels and Hitler feared that a massacre of German women calling for the release of their husbands might cause domestic unrest."

Anton

"You're right. Firing on the women could trigger anti-Nazi protests in Berlin and other cities undermining the domestic unity needed for the war. Germans might even question the legitimacy of the Nazi regime."

Anton

"Especially since this comes right after the disaster at Stalingrad, which has likely weakened dedication to the Party. Party leaders are worried. They're coming down hard on what they call defeatists, anyone who voices doubt that Germany will win the war."

Derek

"And Goebbels also feared that if the protest did not end immediately, all the publicity spread by the international press stationed in Berlin and by word of mouth would anger many Germans. They might even ask: what has happened to the deported Jews? Hitler and Goebbels do not want their Jewish deportation to generate public discussion. Releasing the Jewish men was the simplest way to end the women's protest which could have had disturbing consequences."

Anton

"Hitler considers it an absolute necessity to maintain high morale among the population. Now that Goebbels has declared total war, Nazi Germany must have the united support of the entire population, which the women's demonstration endangered."

Derek

"Be careful not to reveal your feelings. Everywhere, especially among the SS and Gestapo, there are devoted Nazis who will report you. Of course, we can still talk to each other. We've been faithful friends since childhood and both of us have come to despise the Nazis."

Anton

"These Nazi criminals will never break our trust for each other and what we now think of them."

Derek

"But please be careful of what you say in front of the other guys in our unit. Hans is particularly dangerous. In one of the raids I had helped a former Jewish classmate to flee the roundup. Hans saw this and threatened to report me. I told him 'go ahead and I will report you for pocketing money and gems from the Jewish apartment. What will your superiors say to an SS man stealing wealth that should be turned over to the state?' He backed down."

Anton

"We know that fanatic Nazis have turned in former friends and neighbors for criticizing the Party and its leaders. Children have even turned in their parents."

Derek

"We're really going to lose this war. No matter how many we kill and capture, the Russians have the manpower to replace their losses. Nor are we able to destroy their capacity to produce armaments. They cleverly moved their factories east where our planes can't reach them. And contrary to everything Nazi propaganda told us about Slavic racial inferiority, Russians fight bravely and, as Stalingrad shows, they're fighting smarter than at the beginning of the war."

Anton

"Invading Russia was a blunder. There was no reason for it."

Derek

"Hitler had his reasons. In *Mein Kampf* he wrote that for the Germans to gain the land to which they are entitled, Germany must expand east into Russia and its border states. He wanted to settle the fertile Russian plains with Germans and exploit Russia's rich resources. I bet even then he envisioned deporting huge numbers of Russians to work as slave laborers in our factories and farms. Hitler was convinced that the Soviet Union would crumble when attacked by the world's mightiest army."

Anton

"Hitler saw the invasion as an inevitable racial war between inferior Slavs and the German master race. It was a law of history that the superior German race would emerge victorious. But despite our victories the Soviet Union is not crumbling."

Derek

"It certainly looks that way. Stalingrad is an ominous sign. It compels us to question Nazi doctrines of the invincibility of the German army and the certainty of German victory. More civilians are now beginning to think that the invasion of Russia was a dreadful mistake."

Anton

"Stalingrad, no doubt, also leads people to question the leadership of der fuehrer whom, we have been constantly told, has infallible military intuition."

Derek

"Goebbels is committed to Hitler's doctrine that the Party must never lose the popularity of the masses. His propaganda machinery works to keep the people loyal. Notice that now the press and radio, of course ordered by Goebbels, say nothing about our momentous defeat at Stalingrad. People must never doubt that ultimate victory is certain."

Anton

"But what happens after America, that industrial giant, mobilizes all its human and material resources to wage total war? No doubt they're now producing an enormous supply of armaments, particularly tanks and planes. American and Russian power together is too much for us. We will be overwhelmed."

Derek

"And British bombing is growing more severe. Just last week the British air force hit Berlin harder than ever. The newspapers say that 600 people were killed and parts of downtown Berlin are in ruins. It will only get worse. Remember Goering's vow that he would take the Jewish name Meir if Berlin were ever bombed. No one is holding him to it, but they do laugh at this fat Nazi."

Anton

"I don't like bringing this up, but how are you personally reacting to our role in rounding up Jews?"

Derek

"We both have been with the Gestapo for two years. For a while we've been assigned to collecting Jews marked for deportation. We break into their homes, give them a few minutes to pack some clothes and medication and load whole families into trucks that take them to detention centers. From there they are moved to railroads and taken to Poland. God only knows what happens to them when they get to Poland. But we know that none return."

Anton

"There are rumors that they are herded into crowded ghettos or they are sent to concentration camps. In either case, from what we hear, they are starved, beaten, and worked often to death."

Derek

"And now there is talk that Jews from all over occupied Europe are being massacred in gas chambers. Auschwitz is mentioned as a major killing center. Knowledgeable people are saying that the thousands of Jews just rounded up in Berlin will end up at Auschwitz. If all of this is true we've been aiding mass murderers in their evil acts."

Anton

"My heart remains crushed for my assistance in removing a prominent Jewish violinist from his apartment for deportation to Poland. Before the war, Goebbels had him thrown out of Berlin's leading symphony orchestra along with other Jewish musicians. Now they wanted him deported. I helped this elderly gentleman onto the truck. He would never survive the horrors that awaited him in Poland."

Derek

"I had the same experience with a top journalist who had been thrown off his paper along with other Jewish writers. The Nazis have achieved their goal of eliminating all Jews from German cultural life. How many talented people have we lost because of these Nazi barbarians! And many of our people have bought Hitler's views on race. They think that ridding the country of all Jews will create a new and better Germany. What nonsense!"

Anton

"But we fell for this race nonsense. The overwhelming number of these deported Jews considered themselves loyal Germans and greatly valued German culture. And their contributions to Germany as physicians, lawyers, writers, scientists, and businessmen was immense."

Derek

"The Nazis were determined to rid the country of all Jews and we assisted them! Not a nice feeling, but what are we to do?"

Anton

"If we say we want to quit the Gestapo they will ask us why. We can't give them the real reason. And if we do provide an acceptable reason they'll send us to the Russian front, where we will kill innocent Russians and get killed ourselves."

Derek

"If we are caught trying to help Jews we will be sent to the camps or immediately executed."

Anton

"How I've changed. When I first joined up with the Gestapo, I was a true believer dedicated to saving Germany from internal enemies, Jews and traitors. Now I am filled with anguish for the suffering I have brought people."

Derek

"I feel the same way. But, I'm sure there are very few like us. Nazi indoctrination has been successful. They have gotten a whole nation to think the way they want us to. And they have the instruments of power to convince or compel us to obey. The German people seem devoted to the Nazis. They do not even question the regime's criminal behavior."

Anton

"The Nazis have all the power. There will not be a rebellion as in the closing days of World War I. We can only hope that we lose the war. I don't like saying that but I see no other way of saving the country from the criminals who control it."

Derek

"I feel the same way. At times my mind is torn by this desire to see the defeat of our country. But we are not traitors when we hope for the defeat of this evil government which is destroying our people's soul. God help us!"

Narrator, "scene 4: the female protesters after Goebbels had ordered the release of their husbands."

Sophia

"We did it! Our men are back with us. It is a joy to have Samuel home. I never realized how much I love him and how important he is to me. But we must moderate our joy.

All our husbands have relatives who failed to get out of the country and were deported to Poland or concentration camps here. Some remaining Jews are kept hidden by good people. They cannot leave their hiding place; there are plenty of people that report hidden Jews to the police."

Emma

"The Nazis were not entirely successful in their drive to immediately eliminate all Jews from Berlin. People are saying that a few thousand had been warned by their factory employers that the SS were coming for them. They fled. But how will they survive; they can't go back to their apartments. There are some people helping Jews, but the police will search the city for them with determination as if these helpless people are grave threats to the country."

Sophia

"And no doubt the police will be filled with great pride for capturing these 'enemies of the fatherland.' What times we live in! We must be very careful now. Don't talk to others about our victory and don't badmouth Nazi leadership. The Nazis have informers everywhere. If we say something against the regime they would be glad to denounce us to the police. You know what that means."

Ida

"That is very important. My brother-in-law, Hans, is a committed Nazi who despises Jews. Knowing him, he will try to get me to say something about our protest that he can report to the police. I will not fall into his trap."

Sophia

"I'm sure we all know people like that, some of them even family. To escape the Gestapo web, we must be vigilant. If people question you about the events, remember: no gloating about how smart and brave we were, no criticism of the government, and no discussion of the torments inflicted on Jews."

Ida

"You're right."

Sophia

"But we did our share. We can take pride that we participated in the only public demonstration against the Nazis and that we were successful."

Emma

"There was another successful protest that should be mentioned. When the Nazis removed crucifixes from school classrooms, large numbers of Catholics in Bavaria protested. Hitler acquiesced and ordered their reinstatement."

Ida

"And many Catholics joined Bishop von Galen's fight against Nazi euthanasia which has deliberately murdered thousands of the physically and mentally disabled. Yes, these Catholics deserve praise, but unlike us, they didn't have to face the SS with guns pointed at them."

Emma

"I would have been even more proud of my church if at the start of the deportation of Jews, bishops had called for mass demonstrations to halt this atrocity on our fellow citizens. Even as the tragedy unfolded before their eyes, the clergy remained conspicuously silent. They stood by and offered no resistance to the Nazis. No doubt they were fearful that the government would punish them—there are priests who have been executed and imprisoned in concentration camps."

Ida

"But I can't help thinking that many clergy just did not care about Jews. Remember Kristallnacht when the Nazis destroyed hundreds of synagogues, wrecked Jewish stores, killed scores of Jews, sent thousands to concentration camps, and imposed a huge fine on the Jewish community? This was before the war and only a few clergy protested. The great majority of our clergy were indifferent or still saw the Jews as infamous enemies of Christ. And they swallowed Nazi propaganda that Jews were dangerous aliens undermining the nation. Nationalism and anti-Semitism subverted any humane feelings."

Sophia

"If we lose the war the German people will have a lot to answer for."

Ida

"If my brother-in-law heard you say that we might lose the war, he would have you imprisoned immediately, maybe even worse. We must be on guard every minute."

Emma

"If the Nazis win they'll no longer have to worry about how the nation feels about our husbands. They'll kill them and maybe even us if we make a scene protesting. I know I sound like a traitor but I hope we lose. A Nazi-ruled Europe would be a tragedy for Germany, Europe, and the world."

Ida

"The Nazis behavior toward Jews says it all."

Sophia

"Our depraved leaders have turned evil into a national policy. The Nazis have disgraced Christianity and repudiated Europe's highest values. For many years, the German people will have to live with this dishonor."

END

THE MIND OF A HOLOCAUST DENIER

Historical Introduction

Anti-Semitism still has the capacity to ignite people's meanest feelings and distort thinking as in the disturbing phenomenon of Holocaust denial. Proponents of Holocaust denial argue that during World War II the Germans had no policy of extermination; the Jews invented the Holocaust to gain world sympathy for Zionism and to wrest enormous indemnity payments from innocent Germans.

In the tradition of earlier anti-Semites, Holocaust deniers intend to inflict maximum pain on Jews, for they know that the Holocaust touches the Jewish soul like few other issues. Virtually all deniers harbor a devouring hated of Jews, which, depending on the circumstances, they either disguise or flaunt. Deniers are obsessed with the stale grotesque theme of an international Jewish conspiracy. For them the Holocaust is still another evil ploy manufactured by Jews in their drive to extend their power and wealth.

Deniers insist that they are scholarly researchers engaged in an honored professional enterprise—marshalling evidence to challenge a traditional view, in this case a widely circulated Jewish lie. They describe themselves as "revisionists" prepared to refute the erroneous and biased conclusions of those who claim that Nazi leadership instituted a policy of systematic murder of Jews. Deniers argue that the evidence for mass shootings of Jews in the Soviet Union and Poland by SS murder squads and the gas chambers in the death camps is untrustworthy as is the testimony of Jewish survivors and the testimony and confessions of Nazis in the various trials between 1945 and 1963. Deniers insist that Jewish testimony is either mistaken or a deliberate lie and that Nazi confessions were obtained through torture, threats, or the hope of a lighter sentence.

There exists a massive and rapidly growing literature on the Holocaust; very able historians, utilizing an array of sources, particularly the official records of the Third Reich, have described the systematic murder of European Jewry. Nowhere in their writings do scholars refer to Holocaust deniers except perhaps as an aside to express their disdain for them. Several countries, including Germany, have made it illegal to propagate this insidious myth.

Narrator, "scene 1: Margaret, Hank, and their college son, Tom, are having breakfast during the Christmas break."

Margaret

"It's so wonderful that you're home for Christmas vacation. Do you still like college?"

Tom

"College is great mom, I like the courses, the professors, and have made good friends with several guys."

Margaret

"And what about making friends with girls?"

Tom

"Plenty of nice girls there, but I'm not seeing anyone in particular. I want to concentrate on my studies. I know we have no college graduates in our immediate family and an engineering degree will bring in a good income."

Margaret

"I'm glad you're going to a Christian college. Study hard and make me proud. And do try to attend church there."

Hank

"Glad you're majoring in engineering Tom, and not history with all those commie Jew professors. Be careful when they teach about the Jews and the so-called Holocaust, that Jewish hoax."

Margaret

"Hank, I do not like you talking like that to Tom."

Tom

"It's OK mom, this is dad's thing."

Margaret

"What he says is terrible."

Tom

"How bad can it be?"

Margaret

"Ask Reverend Stuart what he thinks about your dad's views on Jews."

Tom

"Does Reverend Stuart talk about Jews in his sermons?"

Margaret

"At times. In commemoration of Holocaust Remembrance Day, Reverend Stuart gave an impassioned sermon on what happened to the Jews under Nazi rule. He called the extermination of six million Jews the greatest crime in world history. And, he said, what a travesty that baptized Christians planned and executed this sin!"

Hank

"And you believe him?"

Margaret

"Of course, I believe him. Reverend Stuart is absolutely right. Killing millions of Jews in gas chambers, in mass executions, by slave labor, or just for sport—what a horror!"

Hank

"Margaret, we've been through this before. I don't deny that some Jews, like other civilians, died because of the fighting. But the numbers were small and you can be sure there was no German policy to exterminate Jews. If you believe this, you have been taken in by Jewish swindlers who milk Germany for reparations."

Margaret

"One of our congregants asked about those people who deny the Holocaust. Reverend Stuart said emphatically that these deniers are wicked people who deliberately spit in the face of Jewish survivors of the Holocaust."

Hank

"The Jews have even gotten to our minister, those unscrupulous bastards. I wasn't there, but if Reverend Stuart talks like that again, I'll walk out."

Margaret

"That's because you have a closed mind."

Hank

"For me and my buddies, the greatest crime in history is still the Jews killing Christ. And they should always be made to suffer for it, along with all their other crimes. Tom, don't listen to your mother and make sure to challenge your professors if they serve as a mouthpiece for Jews."

Tom

"I remember everything you've told me since I was a kid and I read all the books and articles you gave me."

Hank (relieved)

"That's great, son. More people like us have to stand up to Jews and communists — we know they control education in the country and are turning colored people into revolutionaries. Well I'm off to work and tonight I have an important meeting with my buddies." *Narrator, "Hank leaves."*

Margaret

"Tom, I didn't get beyond high school. But I read books and watch documentaries on television. Your father's thinking is based completely on hate, not facts."

Tom

"Am I to go against my father and tell him that, especially since I'm not sure he's wrong?"

Margaret

"College is supposed to teach you to think. If after studying the facts, you see that his beliefs are all vicious lies, tell him that you can't accept his views."

Tom

"This will cause a great rift between dad and me."

Margaret

"Did you know that the group your father is meeting with tonight call themselves the Aryan Vanguard? I don't know much about them, but I do know that they constantly denounce Jews and admire Nazi beliefs. Please promise me that you'll have nothing to do with them."

Tom

"I promise, mom. But I cannot just dismiss what dad has been teaching me. He feels that the Jews, together with the blacks whom they manipulate, are trying to take over the country."

Margaret

"That is more nonsense! Reverend Stuart emphasized that Jews suffered so much throughout history because of the myths and lies spread by anti-Semites. I don't want you included with these vile people. I would hate to have you feel the kind of hatred that consumes your father."

Narrator, "scene 2: Tom and his mother at the end of his first year."

Margaret

"It's always wonderful to have you home even if only for the summer. I'm so proud of you, finishing your first year and with excellent grades."

Tom

"The "A" in calculus really boosted my confidence. I know I'll be able to do well in engineering courses."

Margaret

"No one in my family or your father's family ever got a college degree. Just keep working hard."

Tom

"I will mom. But I'm afraid that I'm going to have an unpleasant confrontation with dad over his attitude toward Jews; he has so much hate in his heart."

Margaret

"As you grew up, I feared that his craziness would lead to this."

Tom

"When Professor Ryan, who teaches my course on Nazi Germany, was discussing the Nazi treatment of Jews, I indicated how certain people do not accept the Holocaust and claim that Jews were a bad influence on Germany. Shouldn't we give fair play to their views?"

Margaret

"Did Professor Ryan ask you how you got these views?"

Tom

"When I said from my father, he looked at me with deep concern. He told the class about all the lies and myths that were spread about Jews over the centuries and that Holocaust deniers are an extension of this ugly tradition."

Margaret

"What was your reaction?"

Tom

"He got me thinking. In a special lecture, he arranged for a visiting professor from Germany to show the class a powerful German film about the Third Reich's persecution of Jews and for a survivor to describe her terrible ordeal toiling as a slave in Auschwitz and fighting to survive. I instantly saw that dad's dismissal of the Holocaust was the kind of hatred, practiced by Nazi murderers. Do I want to share in this hatred? I asked myself. I wanted no part of it."

Margaret

"Tom, good for you. I'm planning to take courses online that will qualify me for a college degree. I will have to work part time to pay for tuition and books. I intend to major in history and to take courses in Jewish studies."

Tom

"Wow, that's wonderful. But why this interest in Jewish history and religion?"

Margaret

"You don't know Sarah Altman, the elderly piano teacher, who is a member of our book club. She has an amazing history, which she hid from us for years. Recently at a meeting of our club, when coffee was spilled on her arm, she quickly rolled up the sleeve revealing numbers branded on her arm."

Tom

'This is what the Nazis did to all inmates in the concentration camps. They were addressed not by name but by number. This was their new and only identity."

Margaret

"We pressed Sarah to tell her story, which she did reluctantly. She was a young girl in Austria when the Nazis deported Jews to a Polish ghetto. She fled. Her parents, both concert musicians, were sent from the ghetto to the gas chambers at Treblinka, a notorious death camp designed to liquidate masses of Jews. After hiding for several months, Sarah was arrested and spent time in several concentration camps. She told us of the beatings, shootings, starvation, unendurable work load, and endless indignities inflicted on Jewish inmates."

Tom

"There are so many horror stories like Sarah's."

Margaret

"Sarah's experience, Reverend Stuart's insights, and your father's bigotry have stirred my curiosity about the history of the Jews, their teachings, suffering, and their extraordinary achievements."

Tom

"I'm glad that you have also become aware of Jewish achievement, a topic stressed by Professor Ryan."

Margaret

"Reverend Stuart said that in the nineteenth century when European countries started to grant Jews citizenship and allowed them to attend university, Jews, particularly German Jews, demonstrated enormous creativity, especially in medicine, math, and science. At the time Hitler came to power, Jews, who constituted only one percent of the population had won 32 percent of Germany's Nobel Prizes—amazing! Reverend Stuart also spoke glowingly of the contribution of Jews to American cultural and intellectual life."

Tom

"I love the idea of you going to college, but when you bring books home on Jewish history, you know how dad will react. I am reluctant to tell him what I've been reading and learning about the Holocaust and the historical persecution of Jews. But I now know that everything he taught me and all the literature he gave me to read have no basis in fact. They are simply designed to promote hatred of Jews."

Margaret

"Certainly, I thought about your father's reaction to my studying about Jews, but I'm a grown woman seeking to get an education. Your father will have to live with it."

Tom

"Mom, my respect for you continues to grow."

Margaret

"I wish your father would overcome his addiction to Jew-hatred."

Tom

"So do I, but I'm not optimistic. For dad, the Jews are a convenient and emotionally satisfying explanation for the world's problems both past and present."

Margaret

"I hear that all the time."

Tom

"He holds Jewish businessmen responsible for unemployment in the United States, calls Jews parasites who live off the labor of others, and insists they have no loyalty to our country. He envisions an America ruled by white Aryans. This is a takeoff on Nazi propaganda."

Margaret

"And he adds something to Nazi doctrines—blaming Jewish intellectuals and activists for promoting the civil rights movement which, he says, has provoked black violence and enabled African-Americans to take over local government in many states. And I'm sure he also holds Jews accountable for his own misfortunes. I heard him say that he couldn't get a loan because the banks and the Federal Reserve system are all controlled by Jews."

Tom

"And like the Nazis, he welcomes the camaraderie he shares with his fellow so-called Aryans. His sense of community is based on group delusion. Also like the Nazis, he sees himself an idealist fighting for a noble cause."

Margaret

"When he attacks Jews, he feels that he is engaged in a struggle against evil. And subconsciously this strengthens his masculinity."

Tom

"Good insight, mom. Fighting the Jewish enemy makes him feel like a real man."

Margaret

"As a caring wife and a good Christian, I try to rescue him from his Nazi-like wickedness, but he only sees me as a wrong-headed and meddlesome female. If all this is true, I don't see how he will change."

Tom

"It's sad, but I'm afraid you're right."

Narrator, "scene 3: Later in the summer."

Tom

"That was a wonderful meal, mom. Nothing like I get in the school cafeteria."

Margaret

"Thanks son, glad you liked it. Now let's just enjoy a cup of tea. No heavy talk."

Hank

"Agreed. I just want to be sure that my son's mind has not been corrupted by commie Jew-loving professors."

Tom

"My professors are all very competent."

Hank

"Did they dare tell you that the Holocaust is a great hoax invented by cunning and greedy Jews to get world sympathy for Israel, and money from Germany which is used to fulfill their plan to dominate international finance?"

Tom

"I'm afraid we're going to have a problem, dad."

Hank

"What do you mean problem? Did the professor attack you when you used the material I gave you to read?"

Margaret

"Please, I don't want to hear an angry argument."

Tom

"Professor Ryan and Peter Kern, a visiting professor from Germany, simply denounced Holocaust denial as an insult to reason and an incitement to hatred."

Hank

"Just what I expected."

Tom

"Dad, it's not easy for me to tell you how wrong you've been regarding the Holocaust. And you are not willing to learn. You always shut off historical documentaries and interviews with survivors that appear on TV. Nor have you read books on the Holocaust written by reputable historians. Your thinking is not only hateful; it's ignorant."

Hank

"Tom, these Jew-loving professors have messed up your head. Their so-called reputable historians are either ignorant of the events or are controlled by Jews."

Margaret

"How can you speak like that about books you've never read? I'm afraid it would make no difference if you read what accomplished scholars have written. Your mind is not open to facts that don't fit your delusional views."

Hank

"I bet these fakes didn't teach you about the *Protocols of the Elders of Zion*, a book written by Jews which provides clear evidence of the Jewish plot to take over the world. Even Henry Ford praised it."

Tom

"Professor Kern gave me a book that he edited. It consists of essays written by German academics that treat anti-Semitism and the Holocaust. The essay on the Protocols describes it as a notorious forgery written in France by someone in the service of the czar's secret police. Jews had nothing to do with it."

Hank

"That essay was written by a Jew, wasn't it?"

Tom

"Professor Kern figured you would raise this kind of argument. He told me to tell you that only one of the essays in the book was written by a Jew, and it dealt with Jewish survivors after the war."

Hank

"Even German professors have been taken in by Jews."

Margaret

"Hank, that's not very smart."

Tom

"What was really painful was the film Professor Kern helped compile. It showed Nazi mobile murder squads, the Einsatzgruppen, rounding up Jewish men, women, and children, herding them to execution grounds, and slaughtering them with machine guns, rifles, and pistols. The naked bodies fell into open pits that sometimes were piled high with thousands of victims—a horrible sight."

Margaret

"Reverend Stuart said that Nazi executioners believed that Jews were evil sub-humans, unworthy of life. Eliminating them was a service to humanity."

Hank

"Those shot were really German prisoners of war that were executed by Russians wearing German uniforms. Or they were Russian partisans and criminals who were guilty of terrible crimes against German soldiers. Germans fought with honor; they did not massacre innocents."

Tom

"You are simply covering up for these mass murderers. They believed, as one assassin wrote in his diary, that the demonic Jews intended to destroy Germany and that he was protecting the Aryan race from the Jewish bacillus." *Narrator: "this diary is documented."*

Hank

"All your so-called evidence comes from Jews who are noted for their lying."

Tom

"Just a few years ago a French priest journeyed to the execution sites in Ukraine and interviewed elderly Ukrainian eyewitnesses to the massacres, including some who were ordered by the Nazis to dig pits and cover the bodies with sand in order to make room for the next batch of victims." *Narrator, "the priest's book is available."*

Margaret

"And your honorable German soldiers massacred children, even babies. Were these children criminals?"

Tom

"One million five hundred thousand children perished in the Holocaust."

Hank (showing irritation)

"I believe none of this rot. What I do believe is that these old, and no doubt poor, Ukrainians were bribed with Jewish money to tell these lies."

Tom

"The Einsatzgruppen massacred some 1.3 million Jews. The commanders kept careful records of the number of executed which they sent back to Berlin."

Hank

"Jews cunningly forged and planted these documents."

Tom

"Absurd, Jews had no access to these Nazi files which were discovered immediately after the war."

Hank

"The professors really did a number on you."

Tom

"The film also includes the testimony of Nazis who witnessed the massacres and pictures taken by German soldiers depicting the shootings. It contains painful recollections of Jewish survivors brutalized by Nazi guards in the concentration camps. When the Allies liberated the camps, they saw thousands of corpses and emaciated inmates on their death bed."

Hank

"Inmates were dying because Allied bombings made it impossible to get food into the camps or they suffered from a typhus epidemic spread by their filthy habits. And I do not believe the words of these so-called Jewish survivors who also spread the lies about gas chambers that have been debunked by numerous authorities."

Margaret

"What you call authorities are not scholars who respect evidence, but Jew-haters who dismiss as fake the overwhelming documentation of the gassing of Jews."

Tom

"Dad, the article in Professor Kern's book describes the installing of the gas chambers, the herding of Jews into them, and the piling up of the bodies to be burned in the specially built crematoria. It includes confessions of Germans who built the gas chambers and camp officials who utilized them."

Margaret

"These facts, and so many other well-documented facts, destroy completely the lie circulated by Holocaust deniers that Jews invented the myth of gas chambers."

Hank

"Nonsense. These confessions were made under torture. The Jews devised the tale of gas chambers in order to disgrace Germany and milk it for reparations, which have enriched them."

Margaret

"Tell me Hank: Why in Germany today can people go to jail for publicly saying that there was no Holocaust?"

Hank

"Another example of the power of international Jews."

Margaret

"If the Jews are so strong, how come they couldn't get one country to bomb Auschwitz's gas chambers and the railroad track leading up to the camp? And why did countries accept only a handful of Jews trying to flee the Nazis?"

Tom

"Good point mom. And the money that Germany gives to Holocaust survivors is a pittance compared to the billions the Germans and their collaborators stole from European Jews, what has been called the greatest robbery in modern history."

Margaret

"And how do you compensate survivors for the murder of their spouses and children?"

Hank

"More rubbish. I'm really upset that college has ruined your thinking about the Holocaust hoax and the Jewish menace. Did your professors point out the wicked beliefs and behavior of Jews how, over the centuries, their wicked religion has taught them to kill Christians?"

Tom

"The belief that Jews were plotting to murder Christians is a fairy tale. The reverse is true. In Christian lands, over the centuries there are numerous accounts of Jews being brutalized and massacred. What has stayed with me is how historically Christians have created myths about so-called Jewish conspirators. In the Middle Ages, zealous clergy propagated the myth that Jews were out to destroy Christendom. In the fourteenth century Jews were accused of starting the Black Plague which devastated Europe. During the plague townspeople, their minds twisted by popular anti-Jewish myths, burned Jews alive in joyous spectacles."

Hank

"More lies."

Tom

"In the nineteenth century, European nationalists claimed that Jews were taking over their country and were even conspiring to take over the world. This myth was widely circulated in the Protocols of the Elders of Zion. Until it was proven to be a forgery, the work was a huge worldwide seller, second only to the Bible. And the Nazis taught that an evil Jewish race was conspiring to destroy Germany. Dad, you Holocaust deniers are in the tradition of these wicked disseminators of lies about Jews."

Hank

"Everything I taught you has gone to waste. My own son is now in the hands of evil Jews and their evil religion."

Tom

"The Jews are not an evil people, and Jewish religion is very ethical. The ancient Jews conceived the idea of moral freedom, the individual's ability and responsibility to choose between good and evil. The Hebrew prophets stressed the obligation to live righteously and to care for the poor and oppressed. These values have motivated Jews over the centuries and in the United States today. Rabbi Stein made this a key point in our discussion."

Hank

''What! You went to the synagogue to speak with that kike! Did he try to convert you?"

Tom

"Nothing like that. I just wanted him to explain the ethical values at the core of Jewish religion."

Hank

"The Jews have no ethical values. They're nothing but liars, cheats, and sinners who threaten Christians and the United States. They've schemed for the colored to get all that welfare money so they could use them to take over the country. I'm going to make that rabbi pay for what he did to my son."

Tom

"What do you mean pay?"

Hank

"You'll see. Now get out, I have to make a call."

Narrator: "Hank makes the call, but leaves the door somewhat open."

Hank

"Mike, it's me, Hank. Remember that plan we had. Well I want to do it a week from Friday. Ten of the boys will meet next Wednesday in the usual place and we'll work out the details. This time we use explosives, not fire. I have the explosives in my basement; just have to put the contraption together. We're not just going after the Jew church. I have good reason to also beat the kike rabbi. I'm going to leave him with a note that will keep him permanently in fear."

Tom

"I'm glad the door was slightly ajar and I could hear my father's words. Blowing up the temple and hurting the rabbi. I have to warn Rabbi Stein."

Detective Riley

"Good morning, Mr. Sinclair. We met once before when your Aryan Vanguard demonstration drew a crowd that went after your swastikas."

Hank

"It's still a free country. We had a right to march. No doubt Jewish conspirators put them up to it."

Detective Riley

"The people in neighboring Clinton are still enraged that you marched through a neighborhood where several survivors lived brandishing Nazi flags."

Hank

"We marched into the Jew neighborhood in order to warn these Yid bloodsuckers not to do here what they did in Germany before Hitler dealt with them."

Detective Riley

"Although they cannot prove it, the Clinton police believe your group set fire to the town synagogue last year."

Hank

"Of course, they cannot prove it. The money-grubbing Jews did it themselves for the insurance money."

Detective Riley

"Enough of this ugly Nazi talk. Several people in our town, including me, have relatives who fought the Nazis and some are buried in our military cemetery. Two of our veterans who helped liberate concentration camps tell unbelievable horror stories that you should listen to."

Hank

"Jewish suffering during the war does not compare with what the Allied bombings did to German civilians."

Detective Riley

"We have a new problem. We were told that you have explosives in your basement with which you intend to blow up the synagogue. I got a search warrant with me and I'll check."

Hank

"Only my son could have told you about the explosives. That damn kid turning against his father."

Detective Riley

"I can't tell you how we learned about the explosives. We also have this note written for Rabbi Stein. I'll read it to you. 'Dear rabbi kike. We are going to blow up your synagogue and beat you even after you cry for us to stop. If the synagogue is rebuilt we will destroy that also, and you'll be beaten again.'"

Hank

"You have no proof that I wrote it."

Detective Riley

"Our forensic expert can determine if it was written on your computer, which I'm taking with me."

Hank

"My son gave you the memo—right?"

Detective Riley

"Can't talk about that now. There's more. One of your guys, hoping to avoid arrest for a federal hate crime, said you were planning to destroy the synagogue. And that you were also helping to organize a nationwide terrorist campaign against Jews, African-Americans, Latinos, and immigrants. We turned his statement over to the FBI. Doubtless they will be examining your computer and phone records and questioning other members of the Aryan Vanguard. If this can be proven you can spend many years in jail."

Narrator, "scene 5, A little later."

Hank

"I'm in real trouble. Detective Riley says I could go to jail."

Margaret

"Yes, you can. Threatening to blow up a synagogue and brutalize a rabbi is no small matter. I always hated your association with these Nazis."

Hank

"The Jews are getting their revenge."

Tom

"If Jews were plotting to blow up a church in town and attack the minister, you and your people would call for stringing them up. Dad, Jew-hatred has messed up your mind, like it did for many Germans."

Hank

"My mind is plenty clear. I know that you told the police about the explosives and you gave them the memo. Just wait; soon I'm going to thrash you for your disloyalty."

Margaret

"If you dare attack my son, you'll have to go through me. And I'll move out. I'll stand by you if there is a trial, but I'm out of here if you still have anything to do with that pack of Nazis."

Tom

"If you don't give up these disgusting views, I will also leave you."

Hank

"The Aryan Vanguard has branches throughout the country. We are Christian soldiers dedicated to saving America from commie Jews and criminal blacks allied to the Jews."

Margaret

"You dare to describe your evil plans as Christian?!"

Hank

"And our leadership is planning campaigns against brown invaders who also threaten our country and civilization. This is a noble cause. If I am sent to jail I will teach white prisoners our beliefs. They will make marvelous recruits."

Tom

"You have one hope. Call Rabbi Stein and tell him how sorry you are, and that you are quitting the Aryan Vanguard, and, have come to reject their views. Maybe, he can get the police to back off."

Hank

"I will never apologize to that kike or reject the Aryan Vanguard's teachings!"

Margaret

"Reverend Stuart says that there's too much hate in our world and Christians should have nothing to do with hate groups that go against Jesus' teachings. And he specifically said that the lies taught by your group promote unchristian hatred. After listening to you, I totally agree."

Hank

"I wish you could think like the women I have met at Aryan Vanguard conferences."

Margaret

"I intend to improve my thinking by enrolling in a major university for an online program leading to a degree. I want to major in history, including the history of the Jews."

Hank

"What! You are turning against your husband like your son has turned against his father."

Tom

"You belong with the Nazis who fled to South America after the war. They never stopped thinking that Hitler was a great man and that his Third Reich was shaping a new and better European civilization."

Hank

"In many ways, Hitler **was** a great man with great ideas."

Tom

"And they raised their children and grandchildren to honor Hitler and Nazi Germany and to regard Jews as an evil race."

Hank

"In my own way, that's what I was trying to do with you."

Tom

"I'm afraid that like them you'll remain a Nazi until you're dead."

Hank

"I am not disloyal like you."

Margaret

"Then there is no hope for you . . . or for us."

Hank

"You don't scare me. There are plenty of women tied to the Aryan Vanguard that share my outlook. Go find yourself a Jew husband. You deserve each other. Nor does prison frighten me. I will always uphold the truths of the Aryan Vanguard. Saving my country from the Jewish enemy is my mission in life."

END

The Mind of an American Jihadist

Historical Introduction

In November 2015, Islamist terrorists launched coordinated attacks in Paris that killed 130 civilians. Appalled Muslim clerics, scholars, and officials in several countries accused ISIS terrorists of corrupting Muhammad's teachings; they called terrorists, 'criminals,' 'barbarians,' 'immoral,' 'madmen,' 'enemies of humanity.' These Muslim critics assert that terrorists resort to a narrow and distorted interpretation of Islam that totally neglects Muhammad's commands that mercy is a religious duty and killing civilian noncombatants a grave sin. But does historic Islam foster contemporary terrorism?

Minimizing a religious explanation for Islamic terrorism, several analysts have emphasized political and socioeconomic causes. Other analysts recognize the role of nonreligious factors, but stress that Islamist terrorism is rooted in and nurtured by a religious culture. They hold that today's militant jihadists did not emanate from a void, but consider themselves faithful Muslims who employ violence for an Islamic cause. There's a close connection between historic Islamic doctrines and traditions and the ideology and practices of al-Qaeda and ISIS. Both terrorist organizations are committed to restoring the power of medieval Islam. Both claim they are fulfilling Muhammad's commands and strategies. Both tell followers that voluntarily performing jihad, that is waging war against unbelievers, infidels who threaten the Muslim community, is the highest religious act that a man can perform. The leaders of al-Qaeda and ISIS and their followers are zealots who believe they have an uncompromising duty to return Muslims to the days when Allah's commands, as revealed to Muhammad, governed Islamic society and foreign infidels came under the authority of the Muslim state.

The early followers of Muhammad, says Bernard Lewis, divided the world "into two houses: the House of Islam, in which a Muslim government ruled and Muslim law prevailed, and the House of War, the rest of the world. . . ruled by infidels. Between the two there was a perpetual state of war until the entire world embraced Islam or submitted to the rule of the Muslim state." Jihadists view themselves as true Muslims resuming the war that began with Muhammad for religious dominance of the world.

Radical Islamists, or jihadists, regard terrorism, which often involves deliberate and indiscriminate killing of civilians, including women and children, as morally justifiable if its purpose is to serve Islam. Suicide bombers are indoctrinated to believe that martyrdom gives their life an overarching meaning and guarantees them a place in Paradise.

Islamists, who will only accept the rule of God and his Prophet Muhammad, are repelled by secular Western democracies because their legal systems neither derive from nor impose God's law. Jihadists regard democratic governments as blasphemous human contrivances that legalize female equality, endorse freedom of religion and expression, and tolerate atheism and homosexuality, practices that undermine belief in the true faith. The rise of militant Islam demonstrates the immense difficulty of transplanting Western democratic principles to people whose history and cultural traditions, particularly religious traditions, do not easily mesh with democracy.

Narrator, "scene 1: Monday, Richard and his father Patrick at breakfast."

Patrick

"We haven't had breakfast together for a very long time. You're always busy with your courses on Islam."

Richard

"I've taken this week off from my studies."

Patrick

"Just relieve me. You're not planning on converting, are you?"

Richard

"No dad. I'm just intrigued with Islamic history and theology and learning Arabic."

Patrick

"It's been two years since you stopped going to NYU. With your superb ability, I thought you would get a degree in neuroscience. That's what you planned for when you were granted that generous scholarship."

Richard

"Right now, all my energies are devoted to studying Islam."

Patrick

"While that doesn't make me happy I won't fight you. But NYU, no doubt, has an excellent Islamic Studies department. Why are you spending so much time with the imam in a local mosque? Is he a recognized scholar?"

Richard

"Imam Khan is very wise and he gives me personal attention."

Patrick

"But with a degree from NYU and then graduate school, you would have opportunities in government and academia. What you're doing at the mosque leads to nothing. What does the imam say about 9/11 and Islamic terrorism?"

Narrator: "Richard to himself."

Richard (to himself)

"Be careful. The last thing I want now is an argument with my dad."

Richard (to his father)

"Neither in his sermons or while working with me does Imam Khan touch these subjects."

Patrick

"This might just be a ruse. Have you ever heard him denounce Islamic terrorism?"

Richard

"Not really."

Patrick

"You know of course my brother, your uncle Andrew, a great guy whom you never got to know, perished in 9/11. Islamic terrorism is a scourge. It would give me great pleasure to see you denounce these dangerous terrorists to your imam."

Richard

"I will study Islamic terrorism and get back to you."

Patrick

"Be sure to study how Islamic teachings inspire terrorism. By the way, whatever happened to Lilah, that bright and attractive Arab girl whom you saw as a senior while you were attending Catholic school and she was going to that elite private secondary school?"

Richard

"I believe she is still at Vassar, but I have not spoken to her in almost three years."

Patrick

"Your mother and I truly liked her, but it's probably for the best that you broke up. After what happened to your uncle Andrew, many of our relatives would not have been eager to welcome a Muslim into the family."

Richard

"That's a non-issue. It never went that far. I know uncle John carries on against Muslims whenever he visits. This makes me uncomfortable. I never respond and at times just leave the room."

Patrick

"I understand, but I wonder why since you started with the mosque, you have never spoken out against these jihadists who engage in mass murder."

Richard

"No doubt some of these jihadists believe that they are serving God."

Patrick

"Richard, I know that! Do you think these suicide bombers who slaughter civilians have Allah's approval?"

Richard

"Dad, this is not a subject I want to discuss."

Patrick

"Talk like that and someone would think that you sympathize with the jihadists' deranged thinking and excuse their evil actions. They would say that Imam Khan has corrupted your mind. Please clear this up for me."

Narrator: "Richard to himself."

Richard (to himself)
"I must get off this topic. I will tell dad what he wants to hear."

Richard (to his father)
"Dad, I have never heard Imam Khan laud terrorism. And I have come to believe that to combat Islamist extremism we must investigate the ways jihadists think and attract followers. Then we can deal with them properly."

Patrick

"I accept that. Will we ever understand why hundreds of young people eagerly volunteer to blow themselves up for Allah? And do they ever feel guilty for the killing of innocents and the misery they bring to the victims' families? And does Islamic religion and tradition nurture their thinking and behavior?"

Richard

Narrator: "Richard to himself."

Richard (to himself)

"Be careful. Do not try to challenge and correct your father."

Richard (to his father)

"Dad, this is what we must investigate."

Patrick

"I really want you to condemn Islamic terrorism in no uncertain terms. But it is obvious that you are uncomfortable talking about the subject. We'll continue the discussion some other time. Something else is disturbing me. I can't help but notice that you seem down. Is there anything bothering you that you want to discuss with me?"

Narrator: "Not wanting to tell his father about what he intends to do, Richard kisses him and says simply: "I'm all right. I love you dad.""

Patrick

"Richard, you haven't kissed me since you were a child. I'm worried that something is not right with you."

Narrator, "scene 2: Tuesday, Amir, a Muslim extremist who induces and trains suicide bombers and Richard, who has taken the name Abdul."

Amir

"Your self-sacrifice is the supreme way of drawing close to God. The words of Muhammad prescribe jihad as an obligation. Our revered Prophet glorified jihad and explicitly prescribed it for both the individual and the collective community. He said that those who did not participate in jihad were hypocrites and sick at heart."

Abdul

"My love for Allah—his name be praised—is overwhelming. Dying serving him is my greatest wish. It gives my life an overarching meaning. But, I am troubled. Aren't Muslims prohibited from committing suicide?"

Amir

"You're right. But you are sacrificing yourself as a holy warrior battling Islam's enemies in a holy war. That is not the same as a disturbed person taking his life to relieve emotional stress. Do your parents know that you are now a Muslim with a Muslim name?"

Abdul

"I thought it best not to tell them."

Amir

"That was wise. That you are a former Christian who has embraced the true faith makes your sacrifice even more inspiring. Muslims will revere you like they do the martyrs who destroyed the World Trade Center. Your martyrdom will draw many recruits to our sacred cause."

Abdul

"You and Imam Khan have been superb mentors. I understand why it is an honor for Muslim devotees to strike at infidels everywhere."

Amir

"You were a devoted student. In three days, you will fulfill your sacred mission. Nothing must distract you from it. Remember that infidels are unclean devils who want to lead us away from Allah. They only cherish the evils of this world and are ruled by satanic governments. All infidels are unbelievers; Muslims must denounce them and their beliefs and regard them as enemies."

Abdul

"You are right. Unbelievers are slaves to life's sins. They value movie and sports' idols, possessions, and alcohol, not God. And women parade in skimpy clothes like whores. In their secular societies, people can do things that Allah strictly prohibits. Sharia, God's law, must be taught in American schools and the government must learn to impose its decrees. That is the only hope for my country or for any country until the creation of an Islamic world state ruled by a caliph. The formation of such a state, an even larger and more powerful caliphate that had ruled Islam in the past, is my fondest hope."

Amir

"You have learned your lessons well. Westerners always speak of human rights and individual freedom, but these are sinful values that lead people to question Allah's laws; also sinful is the Western democratic idea that citizens can enact laws for their society. A legitimate legal system comes not from the people but only from God."

Abdul

"Again, you are right Amir. Islamic law is an incontrovertible truth perfectly suited for all nations. Allah's revelation is unchanging. Humans can neither neglect it nor revise it. Islam requires nothing from the West, no philosophy, no art, no political systems. We have received perfection from God. We do not want the West's heretical ideas that challenge the Prophet's eternal truths. We are required never to alter but only to obey these truths which originate with Allah."

Amir

"Very good. In today's world, as in the past, Islam is the absolute solution. It is the aim of our movement to Islamicize the world."

Abdul

"Defeat by Islam provides infidels with a great opportunity —surrendering their unholy beliefs, embracing Islam, and gaining salvation."

Amir

"This is a profound insight. I praise you for your growing wisdom."

Abdul

"When I leave my house with the bomb strapped on, you will be there—right?"

Amir

"I regret that duties to our cause force Imam Khan and me to leave the country tomorrow. But I have total confidence that you will fulfill your duty to Allah. Remember that you are not forced to do this. You are one of many volunteers driven by an all-consuming faith. You are committing jihad in behalf of Allah."

Abdul

"I relish the opportunity for martyrdom and gaining vengeance for the years of humiliation and exploitation suffered by Muslims at the hands of Westerners. Westerners are responsible for all the evil and troubles that burden our Islamic society. Yet, I must admit that blowing up a crowded subway car, probably with a number of children on it, causes me anguish. I was expecting you to see me off with comforting words."

Amir

"In the next two days make certain to read Muhammad's divinely inspired words about the duty of jihad, the greatness of God, and the eternal bliss that awaits you in Paradise. This will strengthen your spirit."

Abdul

"I am constantly inspired by our Prophet's words and actions. They deepen my love for Allah and my willingness to sacrifice myself for him."

Amir

"Remember also that the American empire is a Great Satan engaged in a crusade against Islam. It aids Israelis in killing Palestinians and makes war on Afghans and Iraqis. You and the other warriors who identify with our holy cause are God's soldiers fighting the armies of Satan who want to crush Islam and engage in acts of genocide against Muslims. Never feel pain for killing infidels; they are evil people unworthy of life."

Abdul

"Yes, I know. I take joy in giving up my life to serve Allah— Allahu akbar, God is great."

Amir

"Unbelievers do not understand that we Muslims are eager to die and join with God in Paradise. Martyrs especially are honored in Paradise. Their heroism and devotion to Allah win us many followers."

Abdul

"I don't want to sound like an oversexed American, but I relish the thought of making love to a variety of attractive and obliging females."

Amir

"That's one of the joys of Paradise."

Abdul

"My spirit is strong. I will not fail to carry out God's will."

Narrator: "Amir embraces Abdul and says—"

Amir

"I have total confidence in you Abdul. I know you will succeed. One day we will meet in Paradise."

Abdul

"That thought gives me great pleasure and courage. You will not regret being my mentor."

Amir

"One final word. You must never reveal your mission to anyone. To do so is an unforgivable sin."

Abdul

"I understand fully. I will do nothing to dishonor God and bar my entry into Paradise."

Narrator, "scene 3: Thursday, Abdul and Lilah, an old girlfriend."

Lilah

"It's been a long time, Richard."

Richard/Abdul

"It certainly has."

Lilah

"I still remember fondly the good times we had before I went to Vassar."

Richard/Abdul

"We were good together. I felt we had something special."

Lilah

"Yes, we did. I don't know if I should say it, but I had fantasized about our getting married someday."

Richard/Abdul

"A Muslim married to a Christian; this would have created problems with both families. That's all history now. Tell me how you're doing at Vassar. I remember you wanted to major in art; I always admired your talent."

Lilah

"I started with art, but quickly switched to history."

Richard/Abdul

"Muslim history and theology, no doubt."

Lilah

"No, most of my courses are in the history of Western Civilization, although my instructors do touch on the Middle East."

Richard/Abdul

"No doubt these instructors are Westerners who distort Muslim history. Your commitment must always be to Islam. Forgive me, but you don't even dress like a Muslim woman."

Lilah (somewhat annoyed)

"You don't like my miniskirt? I thought my looking good would please you."

Richard/Abdul

"In some Muslim lands, the morality police would beat you and throw you in jail for violating Sharia law."

Lilah

"Much of Sharia law is hateful to me. It demeans women. Making women subservient to men and restricting their education and employment opportunities are abhorrent traditions that have no place in the modern world."

Richard/Abdul

"Some would argue that Sharia law strengthens women's roles as wives and mothers. It protects the family and women's honor."

Lilah

"I hope I am not hearing you right, but it seems that you, a Christian, support Sharia law. I could not live in a country that brutalizes homosexuals and views women as a man's possession, shackling them with repugnant restrictions. With all its faults America is a wonderful place! In addition to its other accomplishments, Western civilization has produced liberating ideas and practices: political and religious freedom, respect for the individual, and, of late, equality for women. The Islamic world has not adjusted well to these modern ideas."

Richard/Abdul

"I trust you go to the mosque regularly and pray often as does your father."

Lilah

"No, I rarely go to the mosque. Nor does my father. He is a top executive with a hedge fund. He considers himself a Muslim, as I do, but he is thoroughly modern. Many of his associates and friends are Christians and Jews."

Richard/Abdul

"Are you saying that you have no interest in historic Islam and that your father prefers associating with infidels, with wicked Zionists, rather than practicing his ancestral faith? To a true Muslim you speak like a heretic who deserves to be punished."

Lilah

"No! Like other moderate Muslims, I want Islam to experience a reformation that will enable it to fulfill its humane potential and to promote peace and good will in the modern world. Enough of this. I doubt if you mean these words, but you sound like a Taliban. Tell me how you are doing at NYU. I know you got a scholarship to study science, but I forget which area."

Richard/Abdul

"Neuroscience."

Lilah

"It sounds like a tough field, but I remember how brilliant you are. How's it going?"

Richard/Abdul

"I've been out of school for two years."

Lilah

"Given your intelligence, I know it was not because you found the work too difficult. I hope it's not a medical problem."

Richard/Abdul

"No, nothing like that. For the past two years, I've been studying Islamic religion and Arabic intensely at the local mosque. This requires enormous time and effort, but I remain totally committed."

Lilah

"I'm astounded. When you were seeing me, a Muslim girl, you never displayed an interest in Islam. How do you explain this obsession?"

Richard/Abdul

"Two principal reasons led me to immerse myself in Islamic history and religion—American intervention in Afghanistan and Iraq, which continues to kill Muslims, and the Zionist theft of Arab land, which has killed, displaced, and impoverished millions of Palestinians."

Lilah

"So the suffering of Muslims today drew you to Islam."

Richard/Abdul

"In part. But more important was my looking for a truth that gives life meaning. Catholicism no longer could do this for me. But then I discovered the holy Koran. Its beautiful words and profound thoughts inspired me like nothing that I had experienced in Catholic school. Muhammad's life and teachings provide a way of life that will heal humanity's ills."

Lilah

"Like believers in fascism and communism, you are searching for certainty."

Abdul

"Certainty yes, but their certainty came from an ideology, a human creation filled with error. I have found the only true certainty in Muhammad's spiritual message, revelations of Allah's absolute truth."

Lilah

"Richard, you sound like you are ready to convert."

Richard/Abdul

"I'm already a Muslim. My name is no longer Richard but Abdul, which means servant of God. I now have devout faith and my life has purpose."

Lilah

"Oh my God! That explains your reaction to Sharia. How have your parents reacted to your conversion?"

Abdul

"I never told them, and I'm sure you will never divulge my secret."

Lilah

"Please don't tell me you support jihadist suicide bombers most of whom are psychologically deranged because of a troubled upbringing. Or they are driven by violent impulses. Killing brings them pleasure."

Abdul

"Your Western psychology is nonsense. I know that some suicide bombers seek martyrdom as a way of relieving psychological trauma. Most martyrs are not rebelling against their parents. Nor is their pursuit of martyrdom due to a troubled youth, poverty, lack of education, or what you call violent impulses. Martyrs know that the world is moving toward a final battle between Muslims and infidels. It is simply a profound belief in Allah and his commands that they are willing to make the supreme sacrifice. Fellow Muslims will forever honor martyrs."

Lilah

"Do you consider yourself a jihadist?"

Abdul

"My mentor says the West wants to dominate the Middle East and crush Islam. What you call terrorism is in reality self-defense against a brutal, powerful, and irreverent enemy. Devoted Muslims want countries, including America, to be governed by Muslims obedient to Sharia, Allah's law. To bring country after country under the rule of Allah is to liberate suffering people from disbelief. There is no nobler mission."

Lilah

"Who is your mentor?"

Abdul

"I cannot say."

Lilah

"What do you mean you cannot say? I fear your anonymous mentor turns young people into terrorists, even suicide bombers. I bet he floods the Internet with his hate and urges the pursuit of jihad."

Abdul

"He just teaches and advises. I voluntarily am going to sacrifice myself for Allah. Oh, I didn't mean to say that; I just blurted it out."

Lilah

"I'm shocked. No wonder you arranged to see me. You wanted to say goodbye. Richard, or Abdul, you must think what you are doing. Don't tell me you are going to strap a bomb on your body and blow yourself up in a crowd like the other jihadist murderers do."

Abdul

"Allah, please forgive me. I did not intend to reveal my mission. It was an accident, a slip of the tongue."

Lilah

"You must tell me the details of what you call your mission."

Abdul

"I swore to my mentor that I would not talk to anyone about the mission. To do so would be defying God."

Lilah

"No doubt your mentor will be with you when you commit this atrocity."

Abdul

"No, he has already left the country. So has Imam Khan who heads my mosque and teaches me Arabic and how to be a devoted Muslim."

Lilah

"Of course they left the country. They fear being identified with the crime. I doubt if your mentor and other big shots in your terrorist organization encourage their own children to become suicide murderers. Richard, I want to keep you from killing yourself and others."

Abdul

"My mind is made up. I do this to serve God. I don't think you can understand the profound satisfaction this gives me. Before embracing Islam, there was no meaning or purpose to my life. Devotion to Allah and the Prophet's teachings have given me a feeling of self-worth and my life an inspiring sense of mission. And I welcome the camaraderie I share with other devout Muslims. My mentor tells me that my dedication will draw more of the faithful to our sacred cause. This gives my life and death a profound spiritual meaning."

Lilah

"This is perverted dedication. You are not serving God by killing innocents, probably even children. Murder for so-called spiritual reasons is a criminal act that demeans all religions, including Islam."

Abdul

"Killing infidels is not a crime; it is how a true Muslim honors God."

Lilah

"Your mentor and your teacher have brainwashed you with their clever anti-Western rhetoric and the promise of Paradise for committing your ghastly violence. You don't realize it, but you are the victim of a sophisticated terror organization that manipulates your thinking and behavior."

Abdul

"I don't expect you to accept or even understand my intense faith."

Lilah

"My instructor told us that there are passages in the Koran that support peace and humane treatment of non-Muslims. Unfortunately, radical Islam ignores these texts but follows other passages that seem to endorse violence and jihadism. Muslim extremists aim to impose their beliefs, not by persuasion, as do Christians today, but by force and terror as in the early days of Islam."

Abdul

"I have no confidence in what Western infidels say about Muslim theology and history."

Lilah

"I can't believe that you support the violent, terrorist acts committed in every Continent by Islamist radicals. You accuse Westerners of disrespecting Islam, but radical Islamists desecrate and set fire to churches, target civilians for murder, and have even justified raping and enslaving girls and strapping them with explosives to be ignited in a crowd. They propagate passages in antique Muslim holy books that curse non-Muslims and teach young people to hate them. Jews, for example, are described as "descendants of pigs and monkeys." A Muslim who abandons the faith can be imprisoned or even executed. And the clergy has called for the death of intellectuals whose writings, they say, are an affront to Islam. All this doesn't trouble you?"

Abdul

"We have valid reasons for attacking Westerners who have abused us and whose beliefs threaten the true faith. And a Muslim who abandons the faith is a vile heretic, who deserves severe punishment, even death. My mentor says that true Muslims would never change the law prescribed in the Koran and other holy texts; this law is perfect."

Lilah

"Perfect indeed! What about traditional Islamic beliefs and practices that teach the natural superiority of men over women and defend slavery, polygamy, and the beating of women? And so-called honor killings of girls and women accused of staining Islam by their behavior are still common in the Muslim world. Every year hundreds of females are victims of this insane practice. Are these examples of your perfect religion?"

Abdul

"You are obsessed with female issues. As I said before, Muslims try to protect girls and women from men who would do them harm and from their own weak natures that would lead them astray."

Lilah

"What about fanatic clergy who tell the faithful that non-Muslims are unworthy of life? Your view of Islam is not mine! Like other thoughtful Muslims, I reject your perversion of Islam into a religion of hatred and bloodshed—into pathological fanaticism."

Abdul

"I can't listen to such talk. A Muslim who bad mouths the faith will pay dearly for these sins."

Lilah

"Many Muslims today, and I am one of them, believe that Islam remains trapped in the Middle Ages. They want to break with medieval religious doctrines and traditions that promote violence, stifle freedom, and suppress women.

And they want to break the stranglehold that rigid and fanatic clergy have over their faith, particularly the education of the young. Enough of this! Now you must tell me when and where this action is to take place."

Abdul

"This is most difficult for me. But talking to someone whom I still feel close to will ease my anguish over the death of children. You must swear by Allah, blessings upon him, that you will remain silent."

Lilah

"Yes, I swear by Allah not to reveal what you are telling me."

Abdul

"If you break your oath to Allah you have no hope of entering Paradise. Instead, you shall be chained, dragged into boiling water, and burned in fire."

Lilah

"Yes, I understand."

Abdul

"On Friday I intend to blow myself up in a crowded subway car. I know it seems terrible to you, but my people are at war with American infidels who seize every opportunity to usurp our lands and defame and crush our God-given faith. I have a spiritual duty to defend Islam against the Great Satan."

Lilah

"A suicide bomber who kills passengers on a subway, how horrible! Think in human terms. Your so-called infidels are parents and students struggling with life's problems. And think about the little children! Think also about what you are doing to your parents. Most Muslims will detest this horrid act and feel shame. This is not martyrdom for a worthy cause; it is simply evil. For me, such cruelty dishonors Islam and brings you disgrace."

Abdul

"I have given much thought to what I'm doing. I love my parents and do not want to hurt them. I get no pleasure in taking the lives of children. But whatever distress I feel is overwhelmed by my love for Allah and my commitment to Mohammad's praise of jihad. Moreover, I have no doubt that I will be welcomed as a noble martyr in Paradise, a world so different from what we experience here on earth. This will be my reward for seeking to revenge the injustice and suffering that America has inflicted on Muslims."

Lilah

"Is there anything I can do to get you to stop this madness?"

Abdul

"No, I am overjoyed to do God's will. There is nothing more to talk about. I hate to say goodbye to you on these terms. Three years ago, I was desperately in love with you, but our lives have changed. Especially my life. Islam gives me great joy and wisdom. Goodbye Lilah, try to remember me and keep your vow."

Lilah

"Richard, I don't know how to say goodbye."

Narrator: "Abdul leaves and says to himself:"

Abdul*(to himself)*

"I should have been more careful. Amir warned me to beware of anyone, however nice, who will steer me away from Allah. No doubt he would have told me to kill her. Could I have done it?"

Narrator: "When Abdul leaves, Lilah rushes to the phone and cries out loud:"

Lilah

"Does Richard really believe a meaningless vow to Allah will keep me from saving the lives of scores of innocent train riders and also his life? I must contact the FBI."

Narrator: "She gets the phone number and dials."

Lilah

"Yes, FBI. This is very serious. Please connect me with someone who deals with Islamist terrorism."

Narrator: "When an agent answers, Lilah tells him:"

Lilah

"I'm a Muslim college student. I know that tomorrow, Friday, a recent convert to Islam is planning to blow himself up in a crowded subway car. You must stop him. I can give you his name and address and any other information you might need, including my name and phone number."

Narrator: "In Abdul's house, the FBI found a hidden suicide vest and explosives. He was apprehended and is awaiting trial for a serious offense—planning to commit a terrorist act in the United States. The trial is imminent."

END

WHITE NATIONALISM: MYTH AND HATE

Historical Introduction

Most hate crimes committed in recent years in the United States have been perpetrated by advocates of radical right beliefs. Included among radical right hate groups are white supremacists who maintain that government and society should be dominated by white people who are culturally superior to African-Americans, Latinos, and other non-whites. At the core of white supremacist ideology is the conviction that the rapid growth of non-whites, manipulated by Jews for their economic and political advantage, threatens white people with extinction.

Among the worst hate crimes committed by white supremacists in recent years were the shooting of nine African-Americans during Bible study in a church in Charleston, South Carolina (2017); the murder of eleven Jews during a Sabbath service in Pittsburgh (2018); and the killing of 22 people and wounding of 24 others, almost all Hispanics, in a Walmart shopping complex in El Paso (2019).

The shooter in the African-American church, Dylann Storm Roof had posted a manifesto on facebook describing how white supremacist websites had ignited his desire to use violence against minorities who threatened the power of white people and the future of their children. Roof, like most white supremacists who commit hate crimes, was not affiliated with hate organizations but acted independently.

Robert Baldwin, who said at the time of the massacre in the Pittsburg synagogue that he was out to kill Jews, had posted anti-Semitic hate comments on the Internet. He blamed a Jewish organization for bringing in Central American invaders "to kill our people." Baldwin is charged with 44 federal hate crimes.

Before his attack in the Walmart shopping center, Patrick Crusius posted an anti-Hispanic and anti-immigration message online in which he claimed that he was inspired by the mass shooting in a New Zealand mosque that killed 51 Muslims. He said that he was protecting America from "a Hispanic invasion."

The phenomenon of white supremacy is growing rapidly in the United States. Advocates, often from the lower classes, say they are struggling against a corrupt elite that runs the government and promotes inequality. In addition to their racism, white supremacists also champion the nationalist doctrine of America First. For them this means securing the border against illegal immigrants, hunting down and deporting illegals, reducing American troops overseas, slashing foreign aid, rejecting American involvement in globalism, including international efforts at climate control, and resisting attempts at gun control.

Narrator, "scene 1: Louise Simmons and her father Dwayne, head of a Virginia branch of Proud White Nationalists."

Dwayne Simmons

"Louise, I'm so glad that our message is getting across to more and more people. I'm sure you noticed all the new faces at our monthly meetings and the enthusiasm they show for our speakers."

Louise

"Yes dad, I'm thrilled with our success."

Dwayne

"Don't forget that Proud White Nationalists has branches throughout the country. I am told that our organization everywhere is growing."

Louise

"You have helped build a national movement dedicated to saving white America from leftists and the minorities they manipulate. These aliens want to displace white people."

Dwayne

"That is my mission. But it won't be realized until we have the political power to rid our country of blacks who have ruined our cities and schools, the Latinos who have invaded our country to get welfare, and Muslim immigrants who want to impose their religious law on us."

Louise

"Don't forget the Jews who are plotting to rule our country."

Dwayne

"And, of course, there's the Jews who control our universities and turn students into communists. When our movement gains power we'll know how to deal with this threat to America. Now we have to get more Americans to join with us."

Louise

"And that's happening. Your decision to use the Internet to win recruits is paying off even more than we expected."

Dwayne

"There's one thing we can do now and I need your help."

Louise

"You can count on me dad."

Dwayne

"You recall, of course, Dylann Roof's attack on a black church in Charleston that killed nine enemies of the white race. I want to repeat his brave act here, hopefully killing more than nine. And with good planning our hero will not be caught the way Dylann was. Remember that Dylann hoped that his act would initiate a race war. An even larger slaughter of blacks would get more whites to join our movement and participate in the race war that would end the demographic threat to white power."

Louise

"Do you have a volunteer who will undertake the assignment?"

Dwayne

"Not yet. I'm hoping you can recruit someone. Can you find a student at the college who seems a loner and is failing his subjects? If you know someone gain his friendship and try to get him to come to our meetings."

Louise

"I know someone who is flunking out for a second time. He appears depressed and seems friendless. I'll work on him."

Dwayne

"How do you plan to do it?"

Louise

"Simple, dad, after I make him think I love him, I'm confident we'll have him."

Dwayne

"Anything that serves our holy cause. Try to win him in three or four months."

Louise

"Piece of cake."

Dwayne

"I know you'll come through."

Narrator, "scene 2: Louise and Mark some three months later."

Louise

"I'm really glad that you have been coming to the meetings of the Proud White Nationalists. What did you think of my father's talk?"

Mark

"He's always been a marvelous speaker. But tonight, he outdid himself. I was enthralled."

Louise

"Did you notice how receptive the audience was, how they cheered his words? I'm so proud of him."

Mark

"I found myself cheering also. Saving our country from Jews, blacks, Latinos, and Muslim terrorists is a vital mission."

Louise

"It certainly is. I'm glad you want to share in this mission."

Mark

"After each of your father's talks, I grow more enthusiastic and more committed."

Louise

"I love to hear you talk like that. Over the months, what did you learn from my father's lectures about the black and Jew danger to our country."

Mark

"I learned that blacks are ruining our cities with drugs and crime. Black men don't look to work; they just hang around and knock up young girls leaving white people to pay tens of millions in welfare for their bastard kids. Young blacks get rich selling drugs, and they try to hook whites on this junk. They lack the mental ability to succeed in school and they ruin schools with their violence. Black gangs are little armies that terrorize our cities."

Louise

"There's more. My father wants to restore and protect the power of white America. He insists that blacks belong to a lower race that is destroying white culture. We want them to go back to Africa or be forced to live in a few areas in the country where they can have nothing to do with white people. And he rightfully says that Texas has been invaded by Latinos who want a free ride with our welfare money. He calls Patrick Crusius who killed 22 Hispanics in an El Paso Walmart a hero. And what about Jews?"

Mark

"After listening to your father, I learned that Jews are undermining American society as they did in Germany before Hitler came to power. They're money-hungry bankers and financial speculators who manipulate the world economy for their own benefit. These parasites control American business, government, the media, and our major universities. Control over the press, television, movies, and higher education gives them the power to infect and dominate our minds."

Louise

"Nicely said. And what about the Holocaust myth?"

Mark

"There was no mass extermination of Jews during World War II. Jews invented the Holocaust myth in order to get money from Germany and to win support for Israel. I agree with your father that Jews are more loyal to Israel than to America and that we should rid our country of these evil, alien people."

Louise

"Again, well said. Don't forget my father blames Jewish liberals for promoting diversity, which denies that white culture is the best in the world. These Jews also promote globalism, which wants us to value the rest of the world more than America. They are transforming America into a degenerate multiracial society. Our movement is determined to make America great again by going back to the days of white power."

Mark

"Yes, I like your sign: DIVERSITY=WHITE GENOCIDE. I also welcome your association with neo-Nazis. These guys have the right ideas and they are tough. They will join Proud White Nationalists in street battles with our enemies."

Louise

"I am certain that you are now one of us."

Mark

"I'm glad you said that. I want to be one of your group because it brings me closer to you. We've been seeing each other for several months. I see us as two people in love ."

Louise

"It'll get better. I have a book for you, *The Turner Diaries*, that you must read. It will strengthen your devotion to the movement. It depicts the rise of the Organization which gains control of California and exterminates blacks and Jews. After it controls the United States, its policy of extermination expands to include all opponents, liberals, and members of the elite. We white supremacists regard the Turner Diaries as the bible of our revolution."

Mark

"Sounds great. I'm eager to read it."

Narrator, "scene 3: Mark and James, his father."

James

"I know you're not eager to discuss how you're doing at college, but give it a try."

Mark

"Dad, I just don't fit in college. The books and the professors bore me. I hate being there. I'm flunking out a second time. I'm afraid I'm a disappointment to you. I'm not at all like Bruce."

James

"Bruce has done remarkably well in college. In May, he'll graduate with a degree in mechanical engineering. Of course, I'm proud of him. But you're also my son and I love you just as much."

Mark

"Thanks dad. At times, I feel like such a failure."

James

"College is not the only path to a successful and satisfying life. You are very good with your hands. People with that talent can find good ways to earn a living; and they often take pride in what they accomplish with their hands."

Mark

"You're right, I like using my hands and am good at it. But with no experience what kind of job can I get?"

James

"I've made some inquiries that I want to talk about with you. A few years ago, I did legal work for a very successful cabinet maker and carpenter. He keeps telling me that he is indebted to me for winning a case that would have cost him a nice sum if he had lost."

Mark

"Cabinet-making is very appealing to me. I really liked the wood shop in high school and was good at it."

James

"I'm thrilled with your positive reaction. He's getting older now and needs help. He said that since you're my son, he's certain that you have the right attitude. He'll train you as an apprentice—with a decent salary, of course."

Mark

"When can I see him."

James

"Every year at this time he vacations in Israel for three weeks."

Mark

"I can't work for a Jew."

James

"What did you say?!

Mark

"I belong to a group called Proud White Nationalists. Its members want to rid the country of blacks and Jews who are enemies of white America."

James

"I'm astonished and infuriated. How long have you been with these white supremacists?"

Mark

"About four months."

James

"You never spoke to me about this insanity. I want you to quit them."

Mark

"I won't do that. Before I joined, I felt a failure and hated myself. I didn't belong anywhere and my life had no purpose. Now I am part of a crew that values me. I have a feeling of camaraderie and a cause that inspires me. The leader's powerful words strengthen my commitment to white nationalism. I wasn't going to tell you, but I'm in love with the leader's daughter."

James

"That's insane. You're completely messing up your life. You've been indoctrinated by vile haters. You have adopted their crude ideas and, no doubt, applaud their cruel behavior. It breaks my heart to see you attracted to a girl who embraces their hate."

Mark

"I won't have you bad mouth her. You just cannot see that we white nationalists are patriots determined to save our nation by reestablishing white power. We are white warriors who want to protect the glory of our race and advance its power, and we have a duty to fight the threat from racial minorities and immigrants."

James

"White nationalists are fanatics driven by irrational and hateful ideas. And they're dangerous. Since 9/11 white racists have violently attacked far more people in America than any other extremist group. In 1995 Timothy McVeigh detonated a bomb that killed 168 people in Oklahoma City. He carried with him pages from the *Turner Diaries* a racist classic that has had terrible influence on young people."

Mark

"You miss the book's inspiring message— the call to arms to save whites from genocide."

James

"I suppose you also praise the white nationalist rally in Charlottesville and the terrorist who killed a young woman ploughing his car into a crowd protesting the rally."

Mark

"Our leader tells us that the woman was a communist who shares blame for the evils committed by communist regimes throughout the world. White nationalists are patriots not terrorists."

James

"Nonsense. Most Americans were disgusted by the white nationalists' march in Charlottesville. So was I. The marchers included skinheads, the Klan, and Nazis who proudly wore swastikas and chanted anti-Semitic hate."

Mark

"Americans have been so indoctrinated by universities and the press that they cannot see that the marchers were trying to save our country."

James

"If our country needs saving, the enemy are the people who marched in Charlottesville. You realize that these right-wing radicals sprout Nazi racism and even praise Hitler as a symbol of white power. At their meetings, racist skinheads, who live for beer and brutalizing minorities, raise the Nazi salute and shout Heil Hitler. Like neo-Nazis, every year these skinheads celebrate Hitler's birthday. These sick fanatics threaten our democracy."

Mark

"Critics of Hitler and the Nazis have been brainwashed by liberals, many of them Jews. What really threatens our country is the genocide of whites planned by minorities and their leftist allies."

James

"I cannot listen to this kind of talk. Rosenfeld is the son of a Holo-caust survivor whose entire family was murdered by the Nazis. He would never take into his business a Nazi sympathizer."

Mark

"I'd rather dig ditches then work for a Jew."

James

"I've had enough. Soon we'll talk again."

Mark

"Anytime. But I am not a race traitor; I will not leave the movement which is a family to me. And I won't give up my girlfriend. I'm devoted to her."

James

"Too bad. Remember what I'm telling you. You're going to pay for this lunacy."

Narrator, "scene 4: Louise and Mark."

Louise

"I'm so glad we're together. If we were not so close I couldn't ask you to do something really important to me and our movement."

Mark

"What is it? I'll do anything for you."

Louise

"Do you remember Dylann Roof, the hero who killed 9 enemies in a black church in Charleston? He expected his action to cause a race war. It didn't happen. We're hoping that the next incident will do just that. We want you to do what Dylann did, but with better results."

Mark

"Are you saying I should shoot up a black church and kill the people praying there?"

Louise

"Don't look at them as innocent people praying to God. Remember what my father said. They are wicked combatants out to destroy our country and displace white Americans. We need brave Americans like you to stop them."

Mark

"Are white nationalists also planning attacks against Jews?"

Louise

"Yes. We have branches in many states. And we're working with American Nazis. They are utterly devoted to Hitler and Nazi teachings. Their big goal is to rid America of

Jews. They honor both Hitler and Robert Bowers who killed 11 Jews in the Pittsburg synagogue."

Mark

"The Jews got what was coming to them. Did Nazi organizations plan the shooting?"

Louise

"No. Bowers acted alone but was greatly moved by the pamphlets distributed by Aryan and Nazi groups and what they write on the Internet. Like us, they are white nationalists who want to unite whites to save us from black and brown aliens who are overrunning the country, and Jews who have been conspiring to dominate our government and economy. Like us these Aryans believe that America is moving toward a racial civil war for which we must be prepared."

Mark

"What happened to Roof and Bowers?"

Louise

"Roof was put on trial and sentenced to death. Bowers was wounded in a gun fight with the police—he shot 3 of them. He says he will plead innocent at his trial."

Mark

"That is not very encouraging."

Louise

"I know this troubles you, but you have nothing to fear. You'll have great support. If you follow our plans, you'll shoot up the church and quickly get away. They'll never find out who you are. And you'll have succeeded against enemies of America. And after your successful operation, we will have the best love-making you could imagine."

Mark

"That alone makes the operation appealing. Tell me what the plans are."

Louise

"Someone we call Sean will teach you how to use an AK-47. When you're ready, he'll drive you to the church. Be sure to wear gloves. The job should only take a few minutes. Then Sean will take you to a safe house where you'll change the clothes which could identify you. Sean will get rid of the clothes and the gun and take you home. Then you'll come to me."

Mark

"My excitement mounts. I never killed anyone. But your father's right. These blacks are not innocents. They are racial enemies, terrorists who threaten the country I love. We have to stop them now."

Louise

"Keep my father's words in your head. They'll strengthen your courage to do what is right and necessary."

Narrator, "scene 5: Mark and his father in the prison visitors' room."

James

"I never could have believed we would be talking in prison. Your mother cries all the time. Why did you do it."

Mark

"Listening to the lectures of the head of the local Proud White Nationalists, I thought I was doing something heroic and patriotic."

James

"Going into a black church intending to kill a lot of people with an AK47 is neither heroic nor patriotic. Things were going wrong in your life that made you lose control and willing to do evil. You needed help. Thank God that men entering the church saw your gun bag and grabbed you before you could shoot anyone."

Mark

"My mission was a failure, but I realize it's better that way."

James

"How did the white nationalists get you to do this?"

Mark

"Actually, it was Louise, the leader's daughter who worked on me. I thought I was in love with her. She made me believe her father's words."

James

"She played on an immature 19-year old to get you to do the white nationalists' bidding. From the beginning, it was her plan to lure you in order to manipulate your mind. And the clever bitch succeeded."

Mark

"This morning I had permission to make a short call on the pay phone. When I spoke with Louise she was hostile. She said she never heard of Sean, knew nothing about an assault rifle or a plan to shoot up a black church. She said the few times we dated meant nothing to her. She cleverly warned that if I said bad things about her father and his organization, I would be antagonizing White Nationalist prisoners. This meant that they would hunt me down wherever they send me. Then she told me emphatically never to call again and slammed the phone down."

James

"Let's see where we go from here. They're certain to find you guilty of a federal hate crime. Had you killed people you could have faced a death sentence. But the penalty for planning to murder people during a church function could be quite severe. I will get you a first-rate attorney, but you are likely to spend years in prison."

Mark

"Dad, I was such a fool."

James

"You were just short of becoming a mass murderer. Slaughtering black people in a church of all places is an unpardonable atrocity. Hooking up with an organization that propagates hate has ruined your life. You could have been a cabinet maker with a future. Now what do you have?

Mark

"My head was not right and I was driven by what I thought was love and by the leader's words. I did not see my behavior as evil. I was convinced I was doing something noble for my country and my race. White Nationalists would laud me as a hero. How could I have been so stupid?"

James

"It hurts me that your mind was disoriented by hateful ideas spread by hateful people, that you were willing to shoot little children and their parents. I should have been more involved in your life. You needed guidance, if not therapy."

Mark

"Will it help that no one was killed?"

James

"Yes, but the prosecution will say that you did not on your own pull back from a planned murderous rampage. Had the three black men not grabbed you and held you prisoner, you would have gone into the church with your assault rifle blazing."

Mark

"It's clear that I cannot escape prison."

James

"But let's hope the attorney can get you less than a maximum sentence, which would keep you in prison for many years."

Mark

"In prison, I'm afraid that when black inmates learn what I tried to do, they will beat or even rape me. And the leader's daughter implied that Aryan convicts will brutalize me if I implicate her father and his white nationalists."

James

"I was afraid of that. Given your crime, it's unlikely that they'll place you in a country club prison. But for your own safety, they might keep you in solitary confinement for a long period. I will talk this over with your attorney.

Mark, your association with this evil organization and what you intended to do infuriates me. But you are my son and you need help. I'll be here for you."

Mark

"Dad, I need you."

END

BIO

Dr. Marvin Perry retired from the History Department of Baruch College, CUNY 25 years ago. His published works include: *An Intellectual History of Modern Europe/ World War II in Europe: A Concise History/ Antisemitism: Myth and Hate from Antiquity to the Present* (co-author)*/ Antisemitic Myths: A Historical and Contemporary Anthology* (co-editor)*/ The Theory and Practice of Islamic Terrorism* (co-editor)*/ Arnold Toynbee and the Western Tradition/ Western Civilization: Ideas, Politics, and Society*, 11th edition (senior author and general editor)*/ Sources of the Western Tradition*, 10th edition (editor). He has begun writing plays, several of them dealing with historical themes.